D1436494

THE OBSERVER'S BOOK
OF AIRCRAFT

The Observer's Books

THE OBSERVER'S BOOK OF

AIRCRAFT

Compiled by
WILLIAM GREEN

With silhouettes by
DENNIS PUNNETT

Describing
154 AIRCRAFT
with 279 illustrations

1968 Edition

FREDERICK WARNE & CO. LTD.
FREDERICK WARNE & CO. INC.

LONDON   ·   NEW YORK

Recommended by
THE AIR SCOUTS' DEPARTMENT
of
THE BOY SCOUTS' ASSOCIATION

7232 0053
Printed in Great Britain

INTRODUCTION TO THE 1968 EDITION

THE twelve months in which this volume of *The Observer's Book of Aircraft* will remain current promise to provide one of aviation's truly historic years. Nineteen hundred and sixty-eight will witness the ogival slender delta wings of the world's first supersonic commercial transports, the Concorde and the Tu-144, leaving the ground for their initial trials; the testing of the Jaguar, the first example of Anglo-French collaboration in combat aircraft development; the appearance of two truly gargantuan transport aircraft, the military C-5A Galaxy and the commercial Boeing Model 747, and it will see the culmination of ten years of pioneering development in the field of V/STOL combat aircraft with the first production deliveries of the Harrier strike and reconnaissance fighter.

These and other of 1968's débutantes are described and illustrated in the pages that follow, but what of the twelve months that have elapsed since the last edition of *The Observer's Book of Aircraft* appeared? The year 1967 certainly saw its revelations from the aeronautical viewpoint, and a number of these were to be seen in the sky above Domodedovo, near Moscow, in July, when the Soviet Union displayed publicly a bevy of aircraft types previously unknown in the West; revelations which added to the growing list of confusing and farcical appellations bestowed by NATO on Soviet aircraft. Thus, the first revealed Russian essay in the field of military V/STOL rejoices in the name of *Freehand*, no doubt much to the amusement of Alexander Yakovlev and his team; the Mikoyan-designed variable-geometry strike fighter is dubbed the *Flogger*, and the multi-purpose MiG-23 fighter, which, as the Ye-266, established remarkable new international speed records in October and November, will be known as the *Foxbat*!

The Soviet Union was not, of course, alone in revealing new military aircraft, for in the United Kingdom the maritime patrol Nimrod began flight trials, in Japan the Shin Meiwa PX-S patrol flying boat reached the test stage, the French flew the variable-geometry Dassault Mirage G strike fighter, and in the U.S.A. combat rotorcraft took a major step forward in September with the first flight of the AH-56A Cheyenne. Civil newcomers included the Beriev Be-30, the Beech 99, the Jetstream, and, further up the size and power scale, the F.28 Fellowship, but perhaps the oddest civil newcomer to appear in the following pages is the Bushmaster—a modernised version of the Ford Tri-Motor of the 'twenties. WILLIAM GREEN

5

AERFER-AERMACCHI AM-3

Country of Origin: Italy.
Type: Light Observation, Liaison and Utility Monoplane.
Power Plant: One Continental GTSIO-520C six-cylinder horizontally-opposed engine rated at 340 h.p.
Performance: Maximum speed (clean aircraft), 191 m.p.h. at 16,000 ft., 168 m.p.h. at sea level (with external stores), 180 m.p.h. at 16,000 ft., 155 m.p.h. at sea level; cruising speed (65% power at 2,976 lb.), 161 m.p.h. at 10,000 ft., 146 m.p.h. at sea level; range (at 65% power), 420 mls. at sea level, 435 m.p.h. at 10,000 ft.; initial climb rate (clean aircraft), 1,750 ft./min.; service ceiling (at 2,976 lb.), 29,300 ft.
Weights: Empty, 2,390 lb.; loaded (clean), 3,200 lb., (with two Minigun pods), 3,680 lb.
Armament: Four or (proposed production) six NATO MA-4A racks under wings each of 330 lb. capacity. Typical loads comprise two MATRA pods each with one 7·62-mm. machine gun and 1,000 rounds, two General Electric 7·62-mm. Minigun pods each with 1,500 rounds, or two Nord AS.11 or 12 missiles.
Accommodation: Pilot and co-pilot or observer in tandem, or pilot and two passengers.
Status: First of two prototypes flown on May 12, 1967. To be evaluated during 1968 by Italian Army as possible replacement for the Cessna O-1.

AERFER-AERMACCHI AM-3

Dimensions: Span, 38 ft. 6 in.; length, 28 ft. 8 in.; height, 9 ft. 0 in.; wing area, 205 sq. ft.

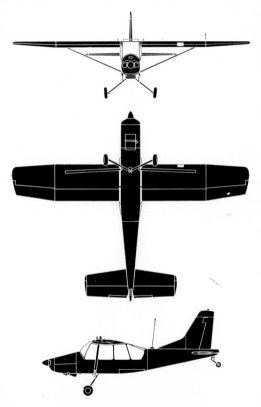

AERMACCHI M.B.326G

Country of Origin: Italy.
Type: Tandem Two-seat Basic Trainer and Single- or
Two-seat Light Counter-Insurgency Aircraft.
Power Plant: One Bristol Siddeley Viper 20 Mk. 540
turbojet rated at 3,410 lb.s.t
Performance: (Trainer at 8,455 lb.) Maximum speed,
524 m.p.h. at 20,000 ft.; maximum cruising speed,
495 m.p.h.; initial climb rate, 6,050 ft./min.; service
ceiling, 47,000 ft.; range (8% reserves), 1,278 mls.,
(with two 52·5 Imp. gal. auxiliary tanks), 1,544 mls.
Weights: (Trainer) Normal loaded, 8,455 lb.; ferry,
9,555 lb.; (armed-one pilot), max. 10,000 lb.
Armament: Four hardpoints each stressed to carry
1,000 lb. and two hardpoints stressed for 750 lb. Six
100-, 250-, or 500-lb. bombs, four 750-lb. M-117
bombs, four 500- or 750- lb. napalm tanks, two Sidewinder AAMs, two Nord AS.11 or AS.12 ASMs, two
M-3 0·5-in., or six SUU 11/A 7·62-mm. gun pods.
Status: (M.B.326G) Prototype flown May 9, 1967.
(Basic M.B.326 with Viper 22-1) In production.
Notes: Prototype M.B.326 flown December 10, 1957.
All current production models have 2,500 lb.s.t.
Viper 22-1 (see 1966 edition). One hundred delivered
to Italian Air Force, eight to Tunisia (M.B.326B),
four to Alitalia (M.B.326D), and seven to Ghana
(M.B.326F). Initial order for 75 placed by R.A.A.F.
for M.B.326H version of which 30th and subsequent of
entirely indigenous manufacture. S.A.A.F to acquire
234 of licence-built version as Atlas Impala.

AERMACCHI M.B.326G

Dimensions: Span, 35 ft. 7¼ in.; length, 34 ft. 11¼ in.; height, 12 ft. 2½ in.; wing area, 208·3 sq. ft.

AERO COMMANDER
TURBO II COMMANDER

Country of Origin: U.S.A.
Type: Light Business Executive Transport.
Power Plants: Two Garrett AiResearch TPE 331-43 turboprops each rated at 575 s.h.p.
Performance: Maximum cruising speed, 280 m.p.h. at 10,000 ft., 270 m.p.h. at 21,000 ft.; initial climb rate, 2,025 ft./min.; service ceiling, 25,000 ft.; range (standard fuel and 45 min. reserves), 1,050 mls. at 270 m.p.h. at 21,000 ft., (with auxiliary fuel—42·5 Imp. gal.), 1,300 mls.
Weights: Empty, 5,783 lb.; maximum loaded, 9,400 lb.
Accommodation: Flight crew of two and six–seven passengers in pressurised cabin.
Status: Original Turbo Commander flown December 31, 1964, with production deliveries commencing June 1965. Improved Turbo II Commander introduced July 1967. In production.
Notes: By comparison with original Turbo Commander, the Turbo II Commander features reduced span, lengthened fuselage nose, clamshell-type fairing doors for main undercarriage members, picture windows and refined engine nacelles. The basic airframe is identical to that of piston-engined Grand Commander which is similar in layout to the earlier range of Aero Commanders.

AERO COMMANDER TURBO II COMMANDER

Dimensions: Span, 44 ft. 0 in.; length, 43 ft. 1½ in.; height, 14 ft. 6 in.; wing area, 242·5 sq. ft.

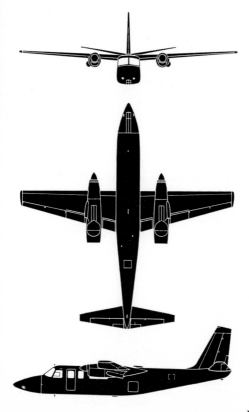

AIRCRAFT HYDRO-FORMING
BUSHMASTER 2000

Country of Origin: U.S.A.

Type: Commercial Utility Transport.

Power Plants: Three Pratt & Whitney R-985-14B radial air-cooled engines each rated at 450 h.p.

Performance: Cruising speed, 140 m.p.h.; economical cruising speed (75% power), 115 m.p.h.; normal range, 700 mls.

Weights: Empty, 6,500 lb.; loaded, 12,500 lb.

Accommodation: Basic flight crew of two and maximum of 15 passengers.

Status: Prototype development. Prototype flown November 1966, and F.A.A. certification scheduled for first quarter of 1968.

Notes: The Bushmaster is essentially a modernised version of William B. Stout's Ford Tri-Motor of the 'twenties, from which it differs primarily in having improved cockpit visibility, trim tabs on all movable control surfaces, larger vertical tail surfaces, and an oleo undercarriage. Employing modern engineering and fabrication techniques, the Bushmaster can accept engines of up to 650 h.p., and is claimed to be ideally suited for bush flying operations in which versatility, a sturdy structure and maintenance simplicity are of paramount importance. The cabin has a total volume of 720 cu. ft., and large freight-loading doors are provided.

12

AIRCRAFT HYDRO-FORMING
BUSHMASTER 2000

Dimensions: Span, 77 ft. 10 in.; length, 49 ft. 6 in.; height, 13 ft. 9 in.; wing area, 900 sq. ft.

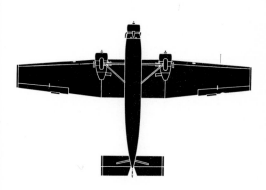

ANTONOV AN-12 (CUB)

Country of Origin: U.S.S.R.
Type: Medium-range Civil and Military Freighter.
Power Plants: Four Ivchenko AI-20K (AI-20M) turbo-props each rated at 4,015 (4,250) e.h.p.
Performance: (AI-20K engines) Maximum speed, 444 m.p.h.; maximum cruising speed, 422 m.p.h. at 32,800 ft.; economic cruising speed, 391 m.p.h.; initial climb rate, 1,960 ft./min.; service ceiling, 33,464 ft.; maximum range (with 22,046-lb. payload and 1 hr. reserves), 2,113 mls.
Weights: Loaded, 119,050 lb.; maximum, 134,482 lb.
Accommodation: Crew comprises five members and maximum freight load is 44,092 lb. Wheeled or tracked vehicles or surface-to-air and surface-to-surface missiles with support equipment may be loaded via rear ramp.
Status: In production. The An-12 freighter derivative of the An-10 commercial transport (see 1967 edition) first appeared in 1959.
Notes: Currently standard Soviet heavy military freighter and paratroop transport, the An-12 also serves with the air arms of Algeria, India, Indonesia, Iraq, Poland and the United Arab Republic. Some commercial examples retain tail gun position, and current models have uprated AI-20M engines. The An-12 has been tested on special skis to suit it for operation from snow in polar regions. The skis are equipped with braking devices and warming equipment.

ANTONOV AN-12 (CUB)

Dimensions: Span, 124 ft. 8½ in.; length, 111 ft. 3½ in.; height, 32 ft. 1¼ in.; wing area, 1,293 sq. ft.

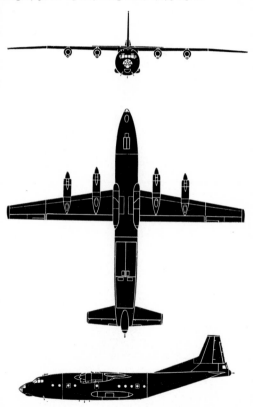

ANTONOV AN-22 ANTEI (COCK)

Country of Origin: U.S.S.R.
Type: Long-range Military and Commercial Freighter.
Power Plants: Four Kuznetsov NK-12MA turboprops each rated at 15,000 e.h.p.
Performance: Maximum speed, 460 m.p.h.; maximum cruising speed, 422 m.p.h.; cruising altitude, 26,250–32,800 ft.; range (with 99,208-lb. payload), 6,835 mls. at 373 m.p.h., (with 176,370-lb. payload), 3,107 mls. at 404 m.p.h.
Weights: Empty equipped, 251,327 lb.; maximum loaded, 551,156 lb.
Accommodation: Crew of 5–6 and cabin for 28–29 passengers between freight hold and flight deck. Freight hold can accommodate three tracked carriers for single Frog or twin Ganef surface-to-surface missiles, self-propelled guns, etc.
Status: First of five prototypes flown February 27, 1965. Two prototypes delivered to Soviet Air Force and three to Aeroflot. First production aircraft (for Soviet Air Force) flown spring 1967. Production for commercial operation envisaged as 30 per year from 1968.
Notes: A developed version for Aeroflot actively under development late 1967 will provide accommodation for 300–350 passengers and 66,140 lb. freight, this load being carried over 1,865 miles.

ANTONOV AN-22 ANTEI (COCK)

Dimensions: Span, 211 ft. 3½ in.; length, 189 ft. 8 in.; height, 41 ft. 0 in.; wing area, 5,166·68 sq. ft.

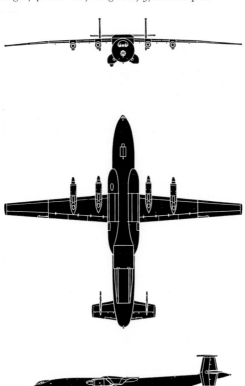

ANTONOV AN-24 SRS. 2 (COKE)

Country of Origin: U.S.S.R.
Type: Short- to Medium-range Commercial Transport.
Power Plants: Two Ivchenko AI-24T turboprops each rated at 2,820 e.s.h.p. and (An-24RV) one Tumanskii RU-19-300 turbojet rated at 1,980 lb.s.t.
Performance: Maximum speed, 335 m.p.h. at 19,685 ft.; maximum cruising speed, 311 m.p.h.; economical cruising speed, 280 m.p.h. at 19,680 ft.; range (with maximum payload—12,125 lb.), 400 mls., (with maximum fuel and 5,372-lb. payload), 1,550 mls.; initial climb rate, 1,480 ft./min.
Weights: Maximum loaded (An-24V Srs. 2) 45,540 lb., (An-24RV), 48,000 lb.
Accommodation: (An-24V Srs. 2) Various arrangements possible for maximum of 50 passengers in high-density layout. (An-24TV) Quick-change version with convertible freight hold with rear-loading facilities, freight conveyor rails, electric hoist, and maximum freight capacity of 12,125 lb. Tip-up seats for maximum of 40 passengers.
Status: An-24V Series 2 in production from January 1968. First prototype An-24 flown April 1960, and second prototype plus five pre-production An-24s completed 1961. First production deliveries 1962.
Notes: An-24V Srs. 2 supplants Srs. 1 which has 2,550 e.s.h.p. AI-24 turboprops. An-24RV (illustrated above) has auxiliary turbojet in starboard engine nacelle, and An-24TV (illustrated opposite) has air-openable rear freight hatch and twin ventral strakes. A military version serves with the Soviet Air Force.

18

ANTONOV AN-24 SRS. 2 (COKE)

Dimensions: Span, 95 ft. 10 in.; length, 77 ft. 2½ in.; height, 27 ft. 4 in.; wing area, 779·845 sq. ft.

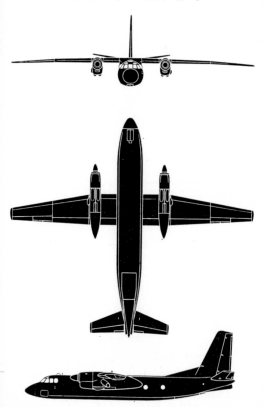

BAC 167

Country of Origin: United Kingdom.
Type: Side-by-side Two-seat Basic Trainer and Light
Attack and Counter-insurgency Aircraft.
Power Plant: One Bristol Siddeley Viper 535 (20-F.20)
turbojet rated at 3,410 lb.s.t.
Performance: (Estimated) Maximum speed, 481 m.p.h.
at 20,000 ft.; initial climb rate (at 10,823 lb.), 3,200 ft./
min.; time to 20,000 ft. (at 10,823 lb.), 9 min.; range
(for navigational training at 8,855 lb. with 10%
reserves), 985 mls.; tactical radius (with four MATRA
rocket pods, 48 Imp. gal. wingtip tank and 7 min. over.
target), 253 mls., (with two MATRA pods, wingtip
tanks, two 75 Imp. gal. underwing tanks), 449 mls.,
(with wingtip tanks and four 75 Imp. gal. underwing
tanks), 628 mls.
Weights: Empty, 5,850 lb.; loaded (pilot training),
7,960 lb., (navigational training with wingtip tanks),
8,855 lb., (two guns, four MATRA pods and tip
tanks), 10,823 lb.; maximum loaded, 11,500 lb.
Armament: Two 7·62-mm. F.N. machine guns with
590 r.p.g., plus four MATRA 155 pods each with 18
SNEB 68-mm. rockets, four pods each with 36 2-in.
rockets, 32 80-mm. rockets, or four 500-lb. bombs.
Status: First flown October 26, 1967. In production.
First deliveries early 1968.
Notes: The BAC 167 is essentially similar to the BAC
145 Jet Provost T.5 (see 1966 edition) but employs a
more powerful engine. BAC 167s are to be delivered
to the Royal Saudi, Sudanese, and the Sultan of
Muscat and Oman's air forces. The Jet Provost T.5
flew on February 28, 1967.

BAC 167

Dimensions: Span, 35 ft. 4 in., (over tip tanks), 36 ft. 11 in.; length, 33 ft. 7½ in.; height, 10 ft. 2 in.; wing area, 213·7 sq. ft.

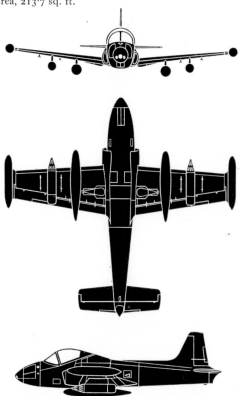

BAC LIGHTNING F. MK. 6

Country of Origin: United Kingdom.
Type: Single-seat All-weather Interceptor Fighter.
Power Plants: Two Rolls-Royce RB.146 Avon 301 turbojets each rated at 12,690 lb.s.t. and 16,360 lb.s.t. with afterburning.
Performance: (Estimated) Maximum speed, 1,500 m.p.h. at 40,000 ft. (Mach 2·27); long-range cruising speed, 595 m.p.h. at 36,000–40,000 ft.; range (with 600 Imp. gal. ventral tank), 700–800 mls.; initial climb rate, 50,000 ft./min.; time to 40,000 ft., 2·5 min.
Weights: (Estimated) Loaded, 40,000–42,000 lb.; maximum loaded, 48,000–50,000 lb.
Armament: Interchangeable packs containing the equipment for two Red Top or Firestreak AAMs, or two retractable boxes each housing 22 Mk. 1 2-in. missiles.
Status: First F. Mk. 6 flown June 16, 1965. Last completed August 28, 1967. Some F. Mk. 3s being brought up to F. Mk. 6 standards.
Notes: Export equivalent of F. Mk. 6 being supplied to Royal Saudi Air Force as F. Mk. 53, this possessing ground attack capability, supplementing interchangeable twin-Firestreak or 44 2-in. FFAR installation with twin 30-mm. Aden cannon in forward portion of ventral pack and two underwing pylons each carrying 1,000-lb. bomb or MATRA 155 pod for 18 SNEB 68-mm. rockets. In addition to 34 F. Mk. 53s the R.S.A.F. is to receive six two-seat T. Mk. 55s (ex-R.A.F. T. Mk. 5s) and has received four F. Mk. 52s (ex-R.A.F. F. Mk. 2s) and two T. Mk. 54s (ex-R.A.F. T. Mk. 4s).

22

BAC LIGHTNING F. MK. 6

Dimensions: Span, 34 ft. 10 in.; length (including probe), 55 ft. 3 in.; height, 19 ft. 7 in.; approximate wing area, 460 sq. ft.

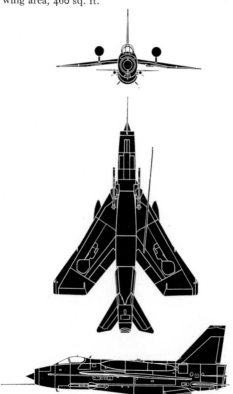

BAC ONE-ELEVEN SERIES 500

Country of Origin: United Kingdom.
Type: Short-to Medium-range Commercial Transport.
Power Plants: Two Rolls-Royce Spey 25 Mk. 512–14 turbofans each rated at 12,000 lb.s.t.
Performance: Maximum cruising speed 550 m.p.h. at 20,000 ft.; economical cruising speed, 507 m.p.h. at 25,000 ft.; range with capacity payload and full reserves, 950 mls.; range with maximum fuel and normal reserves, 1,650 mls.
Weights: Basic, 53,995 lb.; max. loaded, 91,000 lb.
Accommodation: Crew of two and maximum of 99 passengers in all-economy class layout.
Status: In production with first deliveries scheduled for autumn 1968. The series 500 aerodynamic prototype (illustrated above) flew for first time on June 30, 1967.
Notes: The Series 500 One-Eleven has been optimised for stages in the 150–400 mile band, and features increases in fuselage length and wing span, and up-rated engines. The first production example is scheduled to fly in the spring of 1968, and the type is to enter service with BEA early in 1969. Earlier versions of the One-Eleven are flying with 17 airlines, and include the Series 300 (see 1967 edition) which, physically similar to the Series 200, has 11,400 lb.s.t. Spey 25 Mk. 511–14 turbofans in place of the 10,680 lb.s.t. Spey 2 Mk. 506s of the earlier model. The Series 400 (see 1966 edition) is generally similar to the Series 300 but has a lower all-up weight for certain U.S. operators.

24

BAC ONE-ELEVEN SERIES 500

Dimensions: Span, 93 ft. 6 in.; length, 107 ft. 0 in.; height, 24 ft. 6 in.; wing area, 1,031 sq. ft.

BAC VC10 C. MK. 1

Country of Origin: United Kingdom.
Type: Military Strategic Transport.
Power Plants: Four Rolls-Royce Conway R.Co.43 Conway Mk. 301 turbofans each rated at 22,500 lb.s.t.
Performance: Maximum speed, 580 m.p.h. at 30,000 ft. (Mach 0·86); normal cruising speed, 518 m.p.h. at 38,000 ft.; range (with max. payload—57,400 lb.), 3,900 mls. at 425 m.p.h. at 30,000 ft.; (with max. fuel and 24,000-lb. payload), 5,370 mls.
Weights: Operational empty, 146,000 lb.; maximum loaded, 322,000 lb.
Accommodation: A maximum of 150 troops in rear-ward-facing triple-trooping seats plus up to 19,040 lb. equipment. For the aero-medical evacuation role up to 78 casualty stretchers plus six medical and two cabin attendants may be accommodated.
Status: In production. First VC10 C. Mk. 1 flown November 26, 1965. Total of 14 ordered (R.A.F. Air Support Command) and first delivery July 7, 1966. Completion of order was scheduled for December 1967.
Notes: A hybrid of the Standard and Super VC10s, dimensionally similar to the former but possessing the uprated engines and fuel-carrying fin of the latter, the VC10 C. Mk. 1 is equipped with a roller freight-handling system and a new integrally machined freight floor which can take up to eight pre-loaded pallets.

BAC VC10 C. Mk. 1

Dimensions: Span, 146 ft. 2 in.; length (including flight refuelling probe) 166 ft. 1 in.; height, 40 ft. 0 in.; wing area, 2,932 sq. ft.

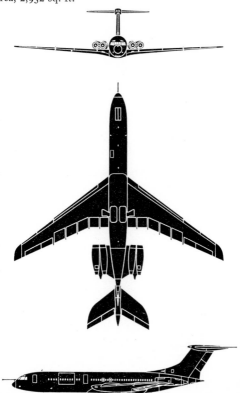

BAC-BREGUET JAGUAR

Countries of Origin: United Kingdom and France.
Type: Single-seat (Jaguar-A and -S) Tactical Support Fighter and Two-seat (Jaguar-B and -E) Advanced Trainer.
Power Plants: Two Rolls-Royce-Turboméca RB.172/T260 Adour turbofans each rated at 4,400 lb.s.t. and 6,600 lb.s.t. with afterburning.
Performance: (Estimated) Maximum speed, 760 m.p.h. at sea level, 1,120 m.p.h. at 36,000 ft. (Mach 1·7); tactical radius (typical lo-lo-lo mission), 370 mls.; maximum ferry range, 2,800 mls.; service ceiling, 46,000 ft.
Weights: Normal loaded, 21,000 lb.; maximum loaded, 28,000 lb.
Armament: Two 30-mm DEFA (Jaguar-A) or Aden (Jaguar-S) cannon and AS.30 or AS.37 Martel ASMs, 1,000-lb. bombs, or rocket pods on five external pylons. Maximum ordnance load of approximately 10,000 lb.
Status: First of seven prototypes scheduled to fly March 1968 with first production aircraft following mid-1970. First 40 aircraft scheduled to enter service mid-1971, initial Franco-British programme covering 300 aircraft.
Notes: Being developed jointly in the U.K. and France, the Jaguar is currently envisaged in five versions: the Jaguar-A and -S being respectively tactical fighter versions for France and the U.K., the Jaguar-B and -E being the training versions for the U.K. and France, and the Jaguar-M being a shipboard version for France.

28

BAC-BREGUET JAGUAR

Dimensions: Span, 28 ft. 0 in.; length, (single-seater) 51 ft. 0 in., (two-seater) 54 ft. 0 in.; height, 15 ft. 0 in.

BAC-SUD-AVIATION CONCORDE

Country of Origin: United Kingdom and France.
Type: Long-haul Supersonic Commerical Transport.
Power Plants: Four Bristol Siddeley/SNECMA Olympus 593 Stage O turbojets each rated at 32,800 lb. and 35,080 lb.s.t. with afterburning.
Performance: (Estimated) Cruising speed, 1,320–1,450 m.p.h. at 50,000–62,000 ft. (Mach 2.0–2.2); range (FAA reserves and maximum payload), 4,155 mls. at mean speed of 1,150 m.p.h. at 50,000–62,000 ft.
Weights: Basic operational, 155,000 lb.; maximum loaded, 367,000 lb.
Accommodation: Maximum high-density seating arrangement for 132 passengers. Typical mixed-class arrangement for 12 first-class and 112 coach-class passengers.
Status: Prototype development. First prototype rolled out on December 11, 1967 at Toulouse, scheduled to fly February-March 1968 with second following mid-1968. First pre-production aircraft scheduled to fly September 1969, and first production aircraft in 1970 with first deliveries 1971.
Notes: Under the terms of an Anglo-French agreement of November 29, 1962, work on the Concorde is shared equally between the two countries. Changes to be introduced by the pre-production aircraft (to which the specification refers) include wider-chord wingtips to improve subsonic handling, a lengthened fuselage, and a new visor and stepped fuselage nose. After two years of airline operation, Stage 1 engines with a non-augmented rating of 35,080 lb.s.t. will be introduced.

BAC-SUD-AVIATION CONCORDE

Dimensions: Span, 83 ft. 10 in.; length, 193 ft. 0 in.:
height, 38 ft. 0 in.; wing area, 3,860 sq. ft.

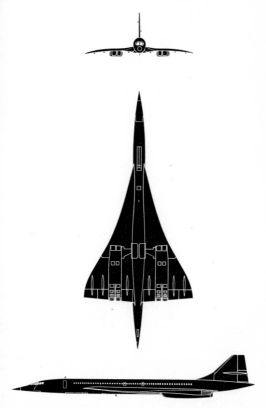

BEAGLE B.121 PUP

Country of Origin: United Kingdom.

Type: (Pup-100) Two- or (Pup-150) Four-seat Light Cabin Monoplane.

Power Plant: One (Pup-100) Rolls-Royce Continental O-200A or (Pup-150) Lycoming O-320 four-cylinder horizontally opposed engine rated at 100 and 150 h.p. respectively.

Performance: (Specification applies to Pup-100 with Pup-150 in parentheses) Maximum speed, 129 (153) m.p.h.; cruising speed at 65% power at 8,000 ft., 112 (138) m.p.h.; initial climb rate, 500 (680) ft./min.; service ceiling, 12,500 (14,500) ft.; range, 600 (576) mls.

Weights: Empty, 970 (1,030) lb.; loaded, 1,600 (1,850) lb.

Accommodation: Side-by-side seating for two persons with dual controls, and (Pup-150) occasional seating for two persons aft.

Status: In production. First prototype (Pup-100) flown April 8, 1967, and second (Pup-150) flown October 4, 1967. First of initial batch of 10 Pup-100s was scheduled to fly January 1968, and first production Pup-150 in April 1968.

BEAGLE B.121 PUP

Dimensions: Span, 31 ft. 0 in.; length, 22 ft. 9 in.; height, 6 ft. 9 in.; wing area, 119·5 sq. ft.

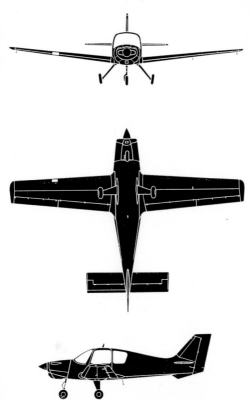

BEECHCRAFT MODEL 60 DUKE

Country of Origin: U.S.A.

Type: Light Business Executive Transport.

Power Plants: Two Lycoming TIO-541-E1A4 six-cylinder horizontally-opposed engines each rated at 380 h.p.

Performance: Maximum cruising speed, in excess of 260 m.p.h.; approximate maximum range, 1,000 mls.

Weights: Maximum loaded, 6,400 lb.

Accommodation: Six persons in tandem pairs of individual seats with small central aisle between seats.

Status: In production. Prototype flown December 29, 1966. First production deliveries were scheduled for late 1967.

Notes: Filling the gap in the Beechcraft line between the Baron and the Queen Air, the Model 60 Duke is a fully-pressurised six-seater, sea level pressure being maintained to an altitude of 10,500 ft., and a cabin altitude of 8,000 ft. is maintained at a cruising altitude of 21,500 ft. A large compartment is available for luggage in the nose, and the entire aft section of the cabin can be converted as cargo space by folding down the rear seats. Consideration is being given to the eventual replacement of the turbo-supercharged piston engines by turboprops.

34

BEECHCRAFT MODEL 60 DUKE

Dimensions: Span, 39 ft. 3¼ in.; length, 33 ft. 6 in.;
height, 12 ft. 3½ in.

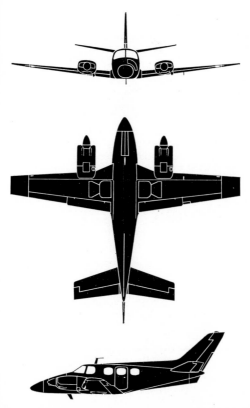

BEECHCRAFT MODEL 99

Country of Origin: U.S.A.

Type: Light Commercial Feederliner.

Power Plants: Two Pratt & Whitney PT6A-20 turbo-props each rated at 550 s.h.p.

Performance: Maximum cruising speed, 250 m.p.h. at 10,000 ft.; initial climb rate, 1,910 ft./min.; service ceiling, 25,000 ft.; maximum range (with 1,800-lb. payload), 975 mls., (with 3,000-lb. payload), 450 mls.

Weights: Empty equipped, 5,675 lb.; maximum loaded, 10,200 lb.

Accommodation: Flight crew of two with maximum of 15 passengers. Seats may be removed to provide cargo space, and movable bulkhead may be installed to provide separate passenger and cargo compartments.

Status: Prototype flown July 1966 with production scheduled to commence spring 1968.

Notes: The largest aircraft yet to be marketed by Beechcraft, the model 99 has been derived from the Queen Air (see 1966 edition) and King Air (see 1965 edition) specifically for the third-level scheduled-service market. It is offered with an optional cargo door adjacent to the standard passenger airstair door for use when operated on all-cargo or mixed-load services.

36

BEECHCRAFT MODEL 99

Dimensions: Span, 45 ft. 10½ in.; length, 44 ft. 6¾ in.;
height, 14 ft. 4¼ in.

BEECHCRAFT U-21A

Country of Origin: U.S.A.
Type: Military Utility and Light Transport Aircraft.
Power Plants: Two Pratt & Whitney PT6A-20 turbo-props each rated at 550 s.h.p.
Performance: Maximum speed, 272 m.p.h. at 21,000 ft.; maximum cruising speed, 254 m.p.h. at 16,000 ft.; long-range cruising speed, 210 m.p.h.; normal tactical radius, 345 mls.; maximum range (with 30 min. reserves), 1,220 mls.
Weights: Empty, 5,335 lb.; loaded, 9,650 lb.
Accommodation: Flight crew of two and maximum of 10 combat troops. Alternative interior configurations for 6–8 personnel, or three casualty litters and three ambulatory casualties.
Status: In production against orders for 129 aircraft scheduled for completion spring 1968. First U-21A delivered May 16, 1967.
Notes: Unpressurised derivative of the King Air (see 1965 edition) ordered "off the shelf" by the U.S. Army, the U-21A features a cargo door forward of the conventional airstair door, and can operate from fields as short as 1,000 ft. in length. Late in 1967, consideration was being given to the re-engining of a number of U-21As with the more powerful PT6A-27 turboprop to permit the aircraft to carry the avionics associated with the Project Crazydog electronic countermeasures equipment.

38

BEECHCRAFT U-21A

Dimensions: Span, 45 ft. 10½ in.; length, 35 ft. 6 in.;
height, 14 ft. 1¼ in.; wing area, 279·74 sq. ft.

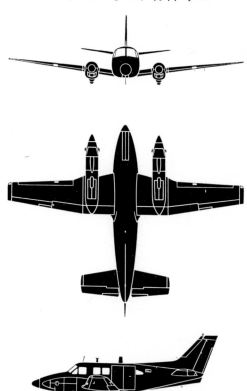

BERIEV BE-12 (MAIL)

Country of Origin: U.S.S.R.
Type: Maritime Patrol and Reconnaissance Amphibian.
Power Plants: Two Ivchenko AI-20D turboprops each rated at 4,000 s.h.p.
Performance: (Estimated) Maximum speed, 380 m.p.h.; normal patrol speed, 200–250 m.p.h. at 5,000 ft.; initial climb rate, 3,000 ft./min.; service ceiling, 37,000 ft.; maximum range, 2,500 mls.
Weights: Approximate loaded, 60,000–65,000 lb.
Status: In production and in service.
Notes: Reportedly flown in prototype form in 1960, the Be-12 is the successor to the piston-engined Be-6 with Soviet maritime patrol units, and follows closely the basic configuration of its predecessor. During 1964, the Be-12 established six officially-recognised international altitude records in the FAI class C.3 Group II for turboprop-powered amphibians. These records included an altitude of 39,977 ft. without payload, an altitude of 37,290 ft. with payloads of 2,205 and 4,409 lb., an altitude of 30,682 ft. with a 22,046-lb. payload, and a maximum payload of 22,266 lb. lifted to an altitude of 6,560 ft. The largest amphibian flying boat currently in service, the Be-12 is of conventional appearance with a magnetic anomaly detection extension protruding from the rear fuselage, a glazed observation position in the nose, and a fully retractable undercarriage.

40

BERIEV BE-12 (MAIL)

Estimated Dimensions: Span, 108 ft. 0 in.; length, 96 ft. 0 in.; height, 23 ft. 0 in.

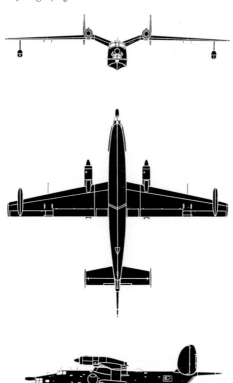

BERIEV BE-30 (CUFF)

Country of Origin: U.S.S.R.

Type: Light Commercial Feederliner.

Power Plants: Two Turboméca Astazou XIV turbo-props each rated at 840 e.s.h.p.

Performance: (Estimated) Maximum cruising speed, 286 m.p.h. at 6,500 ft.; range (maximum payload—2,860 lb.), 350 mls., (maximum fuel and 1,500-lb. payload), 810 mls.

Weights: Normal loaded, 12,566 lb.

Accommodation: Flight crew of two with normal seating for 15 passengers and alternative high-density arrangement for maximum of 20 passengers.

Status: First prototype flown March 3, 1967. Series production expected to commence 1969.

Notes: Designed specifically for use by Aeroflot as a local-service airliner, the Be-30 has been developed by the G. M. Beriev design bureau in close collaboration with that of Oleg K. Antonov, and initial flight trials with the first prototype have been conducted with 740 h.p. ASh-21 air-cooled radial engines. The second prototype is reportedly powered by the Astazou XII, but production aircraft are expected to be powered by a licence-manufactured version of the Astazou XIV. The two turboprops are interconnected so that, in the event of the failure of one power plant, the remaining operational engine drives both airscrews. The Be-30 is the first landplane to be developed by Beriev's design bureau.

BERIEV BE-30 (CUFF)

Dimensions: Span, 55 ft. 9¼ in.; length, 50 ft. 10¼ in.; height, 18 ft. 3¼ in.; wing area, 344·445 sq. ft.

BOEING MODEL 727-200

Country of Origin: U.S.A.

Type: Short- and Medium-range Commercial Transport.

Power Plants: Three Pratt & Whitney JT8D-7 turbofans each rated at 14,000 lb.s.t.

Performance: (Estimated) Maximum cruising speed, 592 m.p.h. at 18,000 ft.; economical cruising speed, 553 m.p.h. at 30,000 ft.; range (with maximum payload—42,275 lb.), 1,130 mls., (maximum fuel and 25,000-lb. payload), 2,300 mls.

Weights: Operational empty, 93,725 lb.; maximum loaded, 169,000 lb.

Accommodation: Alternative arrangements available for 179 passengers in high-density configuration, 180 tourist-class passengers, 163 tourist-class passengers, or 14 first-class and 130 tourist-class passengers.

Status: In production. First Model 727-200 flew July 27, 1967, and first deliveries (to Northeast) were scheduled for December 1967.

Notes: The Model 727-200 is a "stretched" development of the basic Model 727-100 (see 1966 edition) to meet the requirements of the high-density commuter-type market, and differs primarily in having two 10-ft. fuselage sections added, one forward and the other aft of the wing. It is anticipated that the 14,500 lb.s.t. JT8D-9 turbofan will be qualified for Model 727-200 installation during the spring of 1968.

44

BOEING MODEL 727-200

Dimensions: Span, 108 ft. 0 in.; length, 153 ft. 2 in.; height, 34 ft. 0 in.; wing area, 1,650 sq. ft.

BOEING MODEL 737-200

Country of Origin: U.S.A.

Type: Short-haul Commercial Transport.

Power Plants: Two Pratt & Whitney JT8D-7 or -9 turbofans each rated at 14,000 lb.s.t. and 14,500 lb.s.t. respectively.

Performance: Maximum cruising speed, 573 m.p.h. at 26,000 ft.; typical cruising speed, 506 m.p.h. at 30,000 ft.; range (with maximum payload—31,931 lb.), 2,080 mls.; initial climb rate, 3,200 ft./min.

Weights: Operational empty, 56,069 lb.; maximum loaded, 108,000 lb.

Accommodation: Flight crew of two and alternative arrangements for 88 passengers in five-abreast seating, 91 passengers in mixed-class (28 passengers four abreast and 63 passengers six abreast) seating, or 113 passengers in six-abreast seating.

Status: In production. First Model 737-200 flown August 8, 1967, with first delivery (to United Airlines) scheduled for January 1968.

Notes: A "long-body" derivative of the Model 737-100, the first example of which flew on April 9, 1967, the Model 737-200 introduced a 6 ft. increase in overall fuselage length, and is also offered in 737-200C freighter and 737-200QC convertible passenger/ freighter versions. Four Model 737-100s and two 737-200s participated in the FAA certification programme in 1967, and 32 Model 737s were scheduled to be rolled out by January 1, 1968, planned production rate being 14 per month by early 1969.

BOEING MODEL 737-200

Dimensions: Span, 93 ft. 0 in.; length, 100 ft. 0 in.; height, 37 ft. 0 in.; wing area, 980 sq. ft.

BOEING MODEL 747

Country of Origin: U.S.A.

Type: Long-haul Large-capacity Commercial Transport.

Power Plants: Four Pratt & Whitney JT9D-3 turbofans each rated at 43,500 lb.s.t.

Performance: (Estimated) Maximum cruising speed, 625 m.p.h. at 30,000 ft. (Mach 0·89); range cruising speed, 575 m.p.h. at 35,000 ft.; range (with 143,000-lb. payload and normal reserves), 3,450 mls. at range cruising speed (with 366 passengers and full cargo hold), 3,600 mls. at Mach 0·89; maximum range, 8,000 mls.; service ceiling, 40,000 ft.

Weights: Empty, 327,000 lb.; maximum loaded, 710,000 lb.

Accommodation: Flight crew of three–four and alternative interior arrangements for 58 first-class passengers and 308 or 336 economy-class passengers in nine- and ten-abreast seating respectively, and economy-class layouts for 446 passengers in nine-abreast seating or 490 passengers in ten-abreast seating.

Status: In production. First Model 747 scheduled to commence flight test programme during last quarter of 1968, with first delivery (to Pan American) in September 1969. Production of 200 planned by December 1972.

Notes: Mixed-traffic (Model 747C) and all-cargo (Model 747F) versions offered with hinged-nose to permit straight-in freight loading. The first Model 747s will be delivered with a certificated gross weight of 680,000 lb.

48

BOEING MODEL 747

Dimensions: Span, 195 ft. 8 in.; length, 231 ft. 4 in.; height, 63 ft. 5 in.; wing area, 5,500 sq. ft.

BREGUET 941S

Country of Origin: France.
Type: Military STOL Tactical Transport.
Power Plants: Four Turboméca Turmo IIID3 turbo-props each rated at 1,500 s.h.p.
Performance: Maximum speed, 279 m.p.h. at sea level; maximum cruising speed, 264 m.p.h. at 10,000 ft.; economical cruising speed, 230 m.p.h. at 10,000 ft.; service ceiling, 26,250 ft.; range (with maximum payload—22,045 lb.), 500 mls., (with maximum fuel and 11,023-lb. payload), 1,616 mls.; ferry range, 3,100 mls.
Weights: Empty equipped, 30,325 lb.; loaded (assault mission) 46,263 lb.; maximum loaded, 58,422 lb.
Accommodation: Crew of two and 40 fully-equipped troops or 24 casualty stretchers.
Status: Experimental programme. Prototype flown June 1, 1961, and last of four pre-series aircraft was scheduled to fly December 1967.
Notes: The Breguet 941S employs the deflected slip-stream, or blown wing principle, in which the slip-stream of the four airscrews baths the entire wing, the trailing edge of which is fitted with extensive slotted flaps. Engines are synchronised to maintain uniform r.p.m., and interconnected so that all airscrews continue to turn in the event of the loss of one engine.
50

BREGUET 941S

Dimensions: Span, 76 ft. 9¼ in.; length, 80 ft. 0 in.; height, 31 ft. 0 in.; wing area, 901·8 sq. ft.

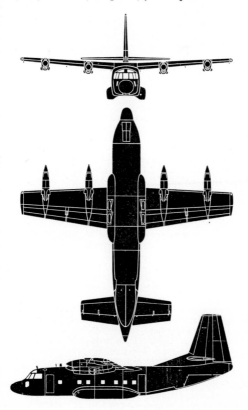

BREGUET 1150 ATLANTIC

Country of Origin: France.

Type: Long-range Maritime Patrol Aircraft.

Power Plants: Two Hispano-Suiza-built Rolls-Royce Tyne R.Ty.20 Mk. 21 turboprops each rated at 6,105 e.h.p.

Performance: Maximum speed, 363 m.p.h. at 19,685 ft.; maximum cruising speed, 342 m.p.h. at 26,250 ft.; long-range cruising speed (at 95,900 lb.), 311 m.p.h. at 26,250 ft.; maximum endurance cruising speed, 199 m.p.h. below 1,000 ft.; loiter endurance (to and from patrol area at 311 m.p.h.), 12 hr. at 195 m.p.h. at range of 620 mls.; ferry range (standard maximum internal fuel), 4,150 mls.; initial climb rate, 2,450 ft./min.; service ceiling, 32,800 ft.; maximum endurance, 18 hr.

Weight: Normal loaded, 95,900 lb.

Armament: Internal weapons bay accommodates Mk. 43 Brush or L.K.4 homing torpedoes, all N.A.T.O. standard bombs, or 386-lb. U.S. or French depth charges.

Accommodation: Crew of twelve, seven of these being accommodated in the central operations compartment.

Status: In production. First of three prototypes flown on October 21, 1961. First production aircraft flown on July 19, 1965. Total orders for 60 aircraft for France (40) and Germany (20).

Notes: Manufactured by consortium of French, German, Belgian and Dutch companies. Atlantic entered service in 1966 with Federal Germany's *Marinefliegergeschwader* 3 and France's *Flottille* 21F.

52

BREGUET 1150 ATLANTIC

Dimensions: Span, 119 ft. 1¼ in.; length, 104 ft. 1½ in.; height, 37 ft. 1¾ in.; wing area, 1,291·67 sq. ft.

BRITTEN-NORMAN BN-2 ISLANDER

Country of Origin: United Kingdom.
Type: Light Utility Transport.
Power Plants: Two Lycoming O-540-E4B5 six-cylinder horizontally-opposed engines each rated at 260 h.p.
Performance: Maximum speed, 168 m.p.h. at sea level; maximum cruising speed, 158 m.p.h. at 6,500 ft.; normal cruising speed (67% power), 154 m.p.h. at 9,500 ft., (59% power), 144 m.p.h. at 13,000 ft.; initial climb rate, 1,220 ft./min.; service ceiling, 17,500 ft.; range (at 59% power), 770 mls.
Weights: Empty, 3,500 lb.; loaded, 5,700 lb.
Accommodation: Cabin can accommodate nine passengers in high-density configuration, and several alternative cabin arrangements available for ambulance and corporate executive versions, the latter having a six-seat interior.
Status: In production. Prototype flown June 12, 1965, first production aircraft following August 20, 1966. First production delivery (to Loganair) August 1967 when initial batch of 30 under construction. Production rate scheduled to attain four per month by beginning of 1968.
Notes: The Islander offers exceptional short-field performance and was originally designed primarily for short-range bush-type operations.

54

BRITTEN-NORMAN BN-2 ISLANDER

Dimensions: Span, 49 ft. 0 in.; length, 35 ft. 7¾ in.; height, 13 ft. 8 in.; wing area, 325 sq. ft.

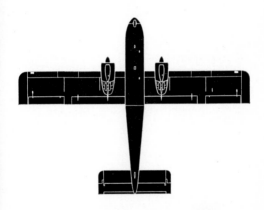

CANADAIR CL-41 (CT-114 TUTOR)

Country of Origin: Canada.
Type: Two-seat Basic Trainer and (CL-41G) Light Attack and Counter-Insurgency Aircraft.
Power Plant: One Orenda J85-CAN-40 (CJ610-1B) turbojet rated at 2,633 lb.s.t., or (CL-41G) General Electric J85-J4 turbojet of 2,950 lb.s.t.
Performance: (Specification relates to CL-41A, figures in parentheses relating to CL-41G without external stores) Maximum speed, 486 (480) m.p.h. at 27,500 (28,500) ft.; initial climb rate, 4,220 ft./min.; service ceiling, 43,000 (42,200) ft.; maximum range (internal fuel), 944 mls., (with six 41·6 Imp. gals./50 U.S. gal. drop tanks), (1,430) mls.
Weights: Empty, 4,870 (5,295) lb.; loaded, 7,300 (7,788) lb.; maximum, (11,288) lb.
Armament: (CL-41G) Up to 3,500 lb. of ordnance on six external pylons, a typical load comprising two 0·3-in. Minigun pods, two 750-lb. napalm tanks and two 250-lb. Mk. 81 general-purpose bombs.
Status: First prototype flown on January 13, 1960. Order for 190 of CL-41A version for R.C.A.F. completed late 1966 when production was continued with 20 CL-41G models for the Royal Malaysian Air Force, these being delivered in 1967.
Notes: A CL-41A adapted to serve as CL-41G prototype first flew in this configuration in June 1964, and this armed version of the basic design (illustrated) has oversize tyres, a reflector sight and armour protection for the crew.

CANADAIR CL-41 (CT-114 TUTOR)

Dimensions: Span, 36 ft. 5¾ in.; length, 32 ft. 0 in.; height, 9 ft. 4½ in.; wing area, 220 sq. ft.

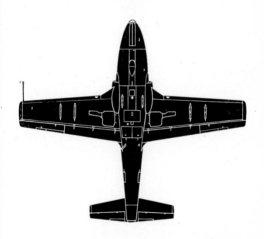

CANADAIR CL-84 DYNAVERT

Country of Origin: Canada.
Type: Tilt-wing V/STOL Research Aircraft.
Power Plants: (CL-84-1) Two Lycoming T53-LTC1K-4A turboprops each rated at 1,400 s.h.p.
Performance: (CL-84-1) Maximum speed, 330 m.p.h.; normal cruising speed, 288 m.p.h.; economical cruising speed, 230 m.p.h.; maximum range (internal fuel), 350 mls., (with two 100 Imp. gal. auxiliary tanks), 830 mls.; maximum ferry range, 2,420 mls.
Weights: Operational empty, 8,100 lb.; maximum loaded (VTOL), 12,200 lb., (STOL), 14,700 lb.
Accommodation: Flight crew of two and space available for 16 passengers on inward-facing troop seats.
Status: Prototype Development. First prototype (CL-84-1) flown May 7, 1965 and completed first transition on January 17, 1966. Destroyed September 5, 1967. Three additional prototypes (CL-84-1A) under construction with first scheduled to commence test programme September 1968.
Notes: CL-84 is proposed as multi-mission aircraft for rescue, utility and troop transport, helicopter escort, surveillance and forward air control roles. Three prototypes currently under construction (CL-84-1A) expected to have 1,600 s.h.p. T53-LTC1S-1A engines.

CANADAIR CL-84 DYNAVERT

Dimensions: Span, 33 ft. 4 in.; length, 47 ft. 3½ in.; height (wing horizontal), 14 ft. 2¾ in.; wing area, 233·3 sq. ft.

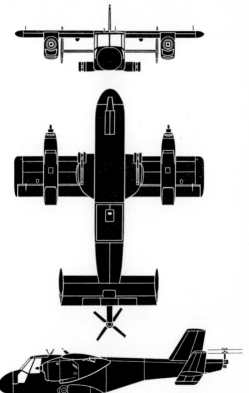

CANADAIR CL-215

Country of Origin: Canada.
Type: Water bombing, Air-sea Rescue and General Utility Amphibious Flying Boat.
Power Plants: Two Pratt & Whitney R-2800-AM2 radial air-cooled engines each rated at 2,100 h.p.
Performance: (Estimated) Maximum speed, 219 m.p.h.; maximum cruising speed, 201 m.p.h. at 5,000 ft.; economical cruising speed (at 35,000 lb.), 139 m.p.h. at 5,000 ft.; range with 45 min. reserves (maximum fuel and 8,000-lb. payload), 1,235 mls. at 144 m.p.h. at 5,000 ft., (maximum payload—12,000 lb.), 345 mls.
Weights: Operational empty (CL-215A), 25,000 lb., (CL-215C) 27,365 lb.; maximum loaded (CL-215A), 41,500 lb., (CL-215C) 35,000 lb.
Accommodation: (CL-215C) Typical seating for 31 passengers, or 36 passengers in high-density arrangement.
Status: In production. First CL-215 flown October 23, 1967. Initial orders call for 20 for the Forestry Department of the Government of Quebec and 10 for France's *"Protection Civile"*.
Notes: Designed primarily for fighting large forest fires by water bombing, the CL-215 is now being offered for a variety of roles. The basic CL-215A water bomber can scoop up 1,200 Imp. gal. of water during its take-off run at 80 m.p.h. The rescue and utility models are designated CL-215B and CL-215C.

CANADAIR CL-215

Dimensions: Span, 93 ft. 10 in.; length, 63 ft. 6½ in.;
height, 27 ft. 2 in.; wing area, 1,080 sq. ft.

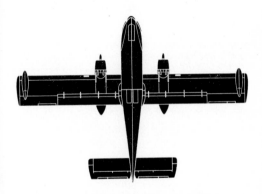

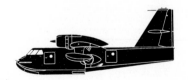

CESSNA T210H CENTURION

Country of Origin: U.S.A.

Type: Light Cabin Monoplane.

Power Plant: One Continental TSIO-520-C six-cylinder horizontally-opposed engine rated at 285 h.p.

Performance: Maximum speed, 234 m.p.h. at 19,000 ft.; cruising speed at 75% power, 197 m.p.h. at 10,000 ft., 223 m.p.h. at 24,000 ft.; initial climb rate, 1,115 ft./min.; service ceiling, 30,200 ft.; range (no reserves), 1,190 mls. at 75% power at 24,000 ft., 1,065 mls. at 10,000 ft.

Weights: Empty, 2,050 lb.; loaded, 3,400 lb.

Accommodation: Pilot's seat standard with optional arrangements for up to five passengers.

Status: In production. Total of 2,186 Model 210 Centurions delivered by August 1, 1967.

Notes: The prototype Centurion was flown in January 1957, production deliveries commencing in 1961. The Models 210H and turbo-supercharged T210H for 1968 production embody minor refinements over the 1967 Models 210G and T210G which dispensed with bracing struts and introduced a redesigned cantilever wing, enlarged tail surfaces, and other changes. The Models 205 and 206 are fixed undercarriage variants of the earlier strutted Model 210, and the Model 206 is produced as the Super Skylane de luxe six-seater and Super Skywagon utility aircraft.

CESSNA T210H CENTURION

Dimensions: Span, 36 ft. 9 in.; length, 28 ft. 3 in.; height, 9 ft. 7½ in.; wing area, 176 sq. ft.

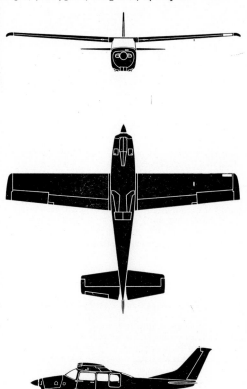

CESSNA MODEL 177 (CARDINAL)

Country of Origin: U.S.A.

Type: Four-seat Light Cabin Monoplane.

Power Plant: One Lycoming O-320-E2D four-cylinder horizontally-opposed engine rated at 150 h.p.

Performance: (Figures in parentheses apply to the Cardinal) Maximum speed, 141 (144) m.p.h. at sea level; cruising speed at 75% power, 130 (134) m.p.h. at 9,000 ft.; range, 755 (780) mls. at 9,000 ft., 825 (855) mls. at 10,000 ft.; initial climb rate, 670 (670) ft./min.; service ceiling, 12,700 (12,700) ft.

Weights: Empty, 1,340 (1,415) lb.; loaded, 2,350 (2,350) lb.

Accommodation: Four seats in two side-by-side pairs.

Status: In production. Deliveries commenced late 1967.

Notes: The Model 177 and Cardinal (the latter being illustrated above and on opposite page) have the same basic configuration and design features, but the latter is the de luxe version with many items standard which are not fitted to the former. These latest additions to the Cessna range of light aircraft feature a new low profile, low-drag design, a fully cantilevered wing, two 4 ft. wide doors forward of the main undercarriage members, weight-saving integral fuel bays in each wing, wide-span flaps and a single-piece all-moving tailplane.

64

CESSNA MODEL 177 (CARDINAL)

Dimensions: Span, 35 ft. 7½ in.; length, 26 ft. 11½ in.; height, 9 ft. 1 in.; wing area, 173 sq. ft.

CESSNA MODEL 421

Country of Origin: U.S.A.
Type: Light Executive Transport.
Power Plants: Two Continental GTSIO-520-D six-cylinder horizontally-opposed engines each rated at 375 h.p.
Performance: Maximum speed, 276 m.p.h. at 16,000 ft.; cruising speed at 75% power, 255 m.p.h. at 20,000 ft.; initial climb rate, 1,700 ft./min.; service ceiling, 26,000 ft.; maximum range (with standard fuel), 1,174 ft., (with optional additional fuel), 1,713 mls.
Weights: Empty, 4,237 lb.; maximum loaded, 6,800 lb.
Accommodation: Flight crew of one or two and standard accommodation of four passengers.
Status: In production. Introduced in August 1967.
Notes: Claimed to be the lowest priced executive twin to offer cabin pressurisation, the Model 421 is essentially a pressurised derivative of the Model 411 which, first flown on July 18, 1962, entered production in 1964, with first deliveries in February 1965. The Models 401 and 402 are lower-powered versions of the basic design (see 1967 edition) which, with 340 h.p. Continental TSIO-520-E engines, are respectively intended for business corporate and third-level feederline operations, the former accommodating five–seven and the latter eight passengers.

CESSNA MODEL 421

Dimensions: Span, 39 ft. 10 in.; length, 33 ft. 9 in.; height, 11 ft. 7 in.; wing area, 200 sq. ft.

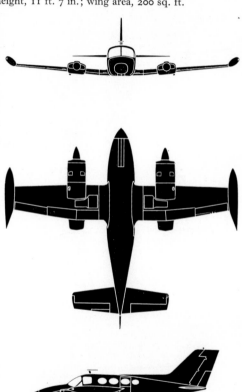

CESSNA A-37B

Country of Origin: U.S.A.

Type: Two-seat Light Strike and Counter-Insurgency Aircraft.

Power Plants: Two General Electric J85-GE-17A turbojets each rated at 2,850 lb.s.t.

Performance: Maximum speed (without external stores), 478 m.p.h. at sea level, (with full external stores), 436 m.p.h. at sea level; initial climb rate (at 12,000 lb.), 6,500 ft./min., (at 8,000 lb.), 10,000 ft./min.; combat radius (pilot only, 12,000 lb. gross weight, cruising at 25,000 ft. with 10 min. single-engine loiter at 15,000 ft. and 5 min. combat at sea level), 85 mls. with 4,700 lb. ordnance, 250 mls. with 3,700 lb. ordnance, and 550 mls. with 1,300 lb. ordnance.; service ceiling, 25,000 ft.; maximum range, 1,400 mls.

Weights: Empty, 5,590 lb.; maximum loaded, 12,000 lb.

Armament: One 7·62-mm. Minigun in fuselage nose and maximum of 4,855 lb. of ordnance on underwing pylons (pilot only).

Status: In production. Thirty-nine A-37As delivered May–September 1967. Contracts for 166 A-37Bs for 1968–69 delivery placed by November 1, 1967.

Notes: The A-37A is modified from airframe of T-37B trainer and has 2,400 lb.s.t. engines. The A-37B, manufactured for the strike role from the outset, has uprated engines and provision for in-flight refuelling. The A-37A joined operations with the U.S.A.F.'s 3rd Tactical Fighter Wing in Vietnam in September 1967. Scheduled to serve with the Vietnamese Air Force.

CESSNA A-37B

Dimensions: Span (over tip-tanks), 35 ft. 10½ in.; length, 29 ft. 3⅓ in.; height, 12 ft. 9½ in.; wing area, 183·9 sq. ft.

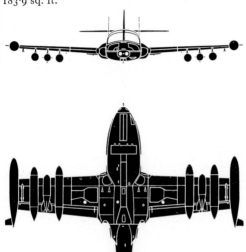

CESSNA O-2

Country of Origin: U.S.A.
Type: (O-2A) Forward Air Control, Observation and (O-2B) Psychological Warfare Aircraft.
Power Plants: Two Continental IO-360-D six-cylinder horizontally-opposed engines each rated at 210 h.p.
Performance: (Without external load) Maximum speed, 200 m.p.h. at sea level; maximum cruising speed, 192 m.p.h. at 5,500 ft.; economical cruising speed, 144 m.p.h. at 10,000 ft.; normal range, 985 mls.; maximum range, 1,300 mls.
Weights: Empty, 2,848 lb.; maximum loaded, 4,300 lb.
Armament: (O-2A) Maximum external ordnance load of 1,400 lb. on four underwing pylons. Typical loads comprise two 7·62-mm. Minigun pods and two pods each containing seven 2·75-in. rockets.
Accommodation: Side-by-side seating for crew of two for operational missions, but pilot and three passengers may be accommodated for liaison tasks.
Status: Contracts for 145 O-2As and 31 O-2Bs were being completed late 1967. Follow-on contract calls for further 47 O-2As. First deliveries to U.S.A.F. effected spring 1967.
Notes: The O-2 is a military version of the commercial Model 337 Super Skymaster, the O-2A (illustrated above and on opposite page) being intended for forward air control, and the O-2B having loudspeakers and facilities for leaflet dropping.

CESSNA O-2

Dimensions: Span, 38 ft. 0 in.; length, 29 ft. 9 in.; height, 9 ft. 4 in.; wing area, 201 sq. ft.

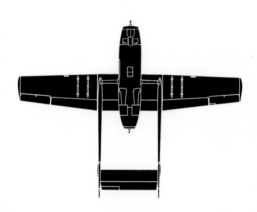

DASSAULT FAN JET FALCON

Country of Origin: France.

Type: Light Executive Transport.

Power Plants: Two General Electric CF700-2C turbofans each rated at 4,200 lb.s.t.

Performance: Maximum permissible speed below 23,500 ft., 425 m.p.h., above 23,500 ft., Mach 0·85 (560–585 m.p.h.); maximum cruising speed (at 20,940 lb.), 535 m.p.h. at 25,000 ft.; economical cruising speed, 466 m.p.h. at 40,000 ft.; range (with maximum fuel, a 1,600-lb. payload, and reserves of 175 mls. and 40 min.), 1,600 mls. at econ. cruise; take-off distance (to clear 35 ft. at 20,940 lb.), 3,200 ft.; landing distance (from 35 ft. at 20,940 lb.), 2,400 ft.

Weights: Empty equipped, 15,212 lb.; maximum loaded, 26,455 lb.

Accommodation: Crew of two and normal seating for eight passengers in individual seats. Alternative arrangements for 10–12 passengers.

Status: In production. Prototype flown on May 4, 1963 and first production example flown January 1, 1965, with 100th delivered on July 20, 1967. Production rate attained seven per month by May 1967.

Notes: Fan Jet Falcon production is shared by Avions Marcel Dassault and Sud-Aviation, and the Business Jets Division of Pan American World Airways has placed orders for 160 aircraft. Military orders include seven for the Canadian Defence Forces and three for R.A.A.F.

DASSAULT FAN JET FALCON

Dimensions: Span, 52 ft. 6 in.; length, 56 ft. 3½ in.; height, 17 ft. 5½ in.; wing area, 452 sq. ft.

DASSAULT MIRAGE M5

Country of Origin: France.
Type: Single-seat Tactical Fighter-Bomber.
Power Plant: One SNECMA Atar 9C turbojet rated at
9,436 lb.s.t. and 13,624 lb.s.t. with afterburning.
Performance: Maximum speed, 875 m.p.h. at sea level
(Mach 1·15), 1,386 m.p.h. at 40,000 ft. (Mach 2·1);
range cruising speed, 594 m.p.h. at 36,000 ft. (Mach
0·9); endurance (maximum external fuel), 4 hr.
Weights: Empty, 13,227 lb.; maximum loaded,
29,760 lb.
Armament: Two 30-mm. DEFA 5-52 cannon plus
more than 8,800 lb. external ordnance. Typical load
for short-range interdiction mission comprises two
1,000-lb., ten 500-lb. and two 250-lb. bombs, plus two
110 Imp. gal. auxiliary fuel tanks.
Status: In production. Deliveries scheduled for 1968.
Notes: The Mirage M5 is an export version of the
Mirage IIIE (see 1967 edition) optimised for the
ground attack role and featuring simplified elec-
tronics. Initial quantity of 50 ordered by Israel
(Mirage M5-J), and 12 ordered by Peru. Claimed to
be the lowest priced combat aircraft possessing Mach
2·0 capability, the Mirage M5 differs from the IIIE
only in having the fire control radar, Doppler and
TACAN deleted, and facilities for the SEPR 844 rocket
motor removed.

74

DASSAULT MIRAGE M5

Dimensions: Span, 26 ft. $11\frac{1}{2}$ in.; length, 50 ft. $10\frac{1}{4}$ in.; height, 14 ft. 9 in.; wing area, 365·97 sq. ft.

DASSAULT SUPER MIRAGE F1

Country of Origin: France.
Type: Single-seat Interceptor and Strike Fighter.
Power Plant: One SNECMA Atar 9K-50 turbojet rated
at 11,067 lb.s.t. and 15,784 lb.s.t. with afterburning.
Performance: Maximum speed, 1,450 m.p.h. at 40,000
ft. (Mach 2·2), 835 m.p.h. at sea level (Mach 1·1);
maximum endurance, 3·75 hr.; service ceiling, 55,000
ft.; range (with maximum external fuel), 2,050 mls.
Weights: Empty, 16,425 lb.; maximum loaded, 24,470
lb.
Armament: (Intercept) Two 30-mm. DEFA cannon,
two MATRA R.530 and two AIM-9 Sidewinder
AAMs, (attack) maximum of 14 250-lb. bombs on
seven external pylons, or mixed conventional ordnance
including two Nord AS.30 ASMs.
Status: Development. First prototype flown December 23, 1966 and destroyed May 18, 1967. Three
additional prototypes ordered May 26, 1967. Production order for 100 anticipated at time of closing for
press, with deliveries to *Armée de l'Air* 1970–71.
Notes: Evolved from the Mirage IIIE (see 1967 edition)
and using some of the systems and much of the fuselage
structure of this aircraft, the Super Mirage F1 has
swept wing, conventional tail, uprated engine and
CSF Cyrano Series 30 radar including both air-to-air
and air-to-ground modes. Variants of the Super
Mirage envisaged include the less sophisticated export
F1A and the tandem two-seat F1B. The Super
Mirage F1 can operate within a 2,600-ft. field length
at average combat weight.

DASSAULT SUPER MIRAGE F1

Dimensions: Span, 27 ft. 9½ in.; length, 45 ft. 10¾ in.; height, 14 ft. 9 in.

DASSAULT MIRAGE G

Country of Origin: France.
Type: Two-seat Strike and Reconnaissance Fighter.
Power Plant: One SNECMA TF-306C turbofan rated at 11,684 lb.s.t. and 20,503 lb.s.t. with afterburning.
Performance: (Estimated) Maximum speed, 840 m.p.h. at sea level (Mach 1·1), 1,585 m.p.h. at 40,000 ft. (Mach 2·4); initial climb rate, 35,000 ft./min.; endurance (maximum external fuel at economical cruise), 8 hr.; service ceiling, 65,000 ft.; ferry range, 4,000 mls.
Weights: (Estimated) Empty, 22,050 lb.; loaded, 35,000 lb.; maximum loaded, 40,000 lb.
Armament: Conventional or nuclear stores on external pylons.
Status: Experimental. First prototype flown October 18, 1967. Development programme towards operational prototype for 1970–71.
Notes: Essentially a variable-geometry equivalent of the Mirage F.2 (see 1967 edition), the Mirage G is currently under development to provide a strike and reconnaissance fighter for *Armée de l'Air* use from 1975. The Mirage G's wing is swept 22° when fully extended and 72° in the full aft position, and translates from full forward to full aft in approximately 20 seconds. Extensive high-lift devices include virtually full-span double-slotted trailing-edge flaps, and two-position leading-edge flaps. Funding in the 1968 budget assures continued development of the Mirage G to the combat prototype stage.

DASSAULT MIRAGE G

Dimensions: Span (minimum sweep), 42 ft. 7¾ in.; length, 55 ft. 1½ in.; height, 17 ft. 6½ in.

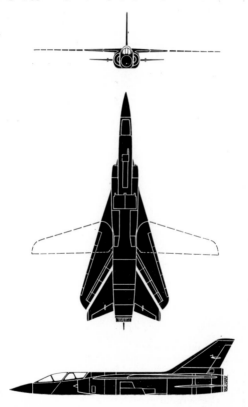

DE HAVILLAND CANADA DHC-5 BUFFALO

Country of Origin: Canada.
Type: Military Tactical and Utility Transport.
Power Plants: Two General Electric T64-GE-14 turbo-props each rated at 3,060 e.s.h.p.
Performance: Maximum speed, 282 m.p.h. at 10,000 ft.; cruising speed at 80% power, 253 m.p.h., at 52% power, 208 m.p.h.; initial climb rate, 2,080 ft./min.; service ceiling, 31,500 ft.; range (with maximum payload—12,780 lb.), 553 mls., (with 8,000-lb. payload), 1,300 mls., (with 4,000-lb. payload), 1,958 mls., (maximum fuel, no payload), 2,142 mls.
Weights: Operational empty, 24,220 lb.; maximum loaded, 41,000 lb.
Accommodation: Crew of three plus 41 troops, 35 paratroops, or 24 casualty stretchers.
Status: In production. First of four evaluation aircraft (CV-7) flown April 9, 1964. Deliveries against initial order for 15 (CC-115) for Canadian Defence Forces' Mobile Command commenced 1967 and scheduled for completion by August 1968. Twelve ordered for 1968 delivery to Brazilian Air Force.
Notes: Originally designed primarily to meet a U.S. Army requirement. Four delivered to this service of which three survivors transferred in 1967 to NASA.

DE HAVILLAND CANADA DHC-5 BUFFALO

Dimensions: Span, 96 ft. 0 in.; length, 79 ft. 0 in.; height, 28 ft. 8 in.: wing area, 945 sq. ft.

DE HAVILLAND CANADA DHC-6
TWIN OTTER SRS.100

Country of Origin: Canada.
Type: Light STOL Utility Transport and Feederliner.
Power Plants: Two Pratt & Whitney PT6A-20A turbo-props each rated at 579 e.s.h.p.
Performance: Maximum cruising speed, 182 m.p.h. at 10,000 ft.; cruising speed (80% max. continuous power), 168 m.p.h.; range cruising speed, 155 m.p.h.; initial climb rate, 1,550 ft./min.; service ceiling, 25,000 ft.; range with 30 min. reserves at 155 m.p.h. (maximum payload—4,250 lb.), 115 mls., (maximum fuel and 2,420-lb. payload), 817 mls.; take-off distance (to clear 50 ft. at max. loaded weight), 1,170 ft.; landing distance (from 50 ft.), 1,050 ft.
Weights: Empty, 5,850 lb.; empty equipped (13-seat utility version), 6,050 lb.; maximum loaded, 11,000 lb.
Accommodation: Side-by-side seats for two crew members. Cabin accommodates 13–18 passengers with 52 cu. ft. baggage compartment.
Status: In production. First of five pre-production aircraft flown May 20, 1965. Approximately 80 completed by beginning of 1968 when production rate was averaging six per month.
Notes: Series 200, available from April 1968, differs from Series 100 in having increased baggage capacity, a lengthened nose, and an 11,400 lb. loaded weight.

DE HAVILLAND CANADA DHC-6
TWIN OTTER SRS.100

Dimensions: Span, 65 ft. 0 in.; length, 49 ft. 6 in.;
height, 18 ft. 7 in.; wing area, 420 sq. ft.

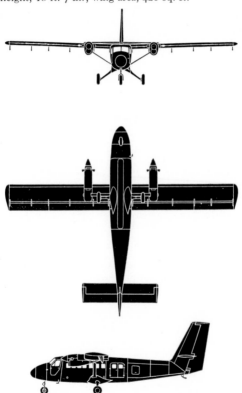

DINFIA I.A.53

Country of Origin: Argentina.
Type: Light Agricultural Monoplane.
Power Plant: One Lycoming O-540-B2B5 six-cylinder horizontally-opposed engine rated at 235 h.p.
Performance: Maximum speed, 134 m.p.h. at sea level; cruising speed (75% power), 115 m.p.h.; initial climb rate, 755 ft./min.; service ceiling, 11,800 ft.; maximum range, 404 mls.
Weights: Empty, 1,860 lb.; maximum loaded, 3,362 lb.
Accommodation: Pilot and tank-hopper, with provision for carrying a second person in tandem on ferrying flights.
Status: Prototype completed for static trials, and second prototype flown November 10, 1966. Second flying prototype completed 1967, and production provisionally scheduled to commence 1968, with planned series of 300 aircraft.
Notes: The first aircraft of Argentine design and construction intended from the outset for the agricultural role, the I.A.53 is of metal construction with light alloy and glass-fibre reinforced polyester plastic covering. The 260 h.p. Continental IO-470-D six-cylinder horizontally-opposed engine is offered as an alternative to the 235 h.p. Lycoming O-540-B2B5. A static test airframe was completed in 1966, and field tests were in progress in 1967 when type certification was anticipated by end of year.

DINFIA I.A.53

Dimensions: Span, 38 ft. 0¾ in.; length, 26 ft. 11 in.; height, 10 ft. 10 in.; wing area, 231·5 sq. ft.

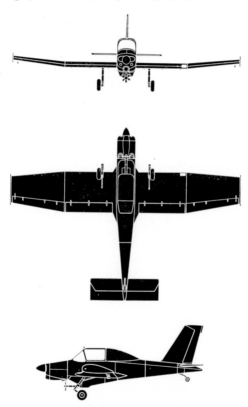

DORNIER SKYSERVANT

Country of Origin: Federal Germany.
Type: Light S.T.O.L. Freighter and Feederliner.
Power Plants: Two Lycoming IGSO-540-A1A six-cylinder horizontally-opposed engines each rated at 380 h.p.
Performance: Maximum speed, 201 m.p.h. at 10,000 ft.; economical cruising speed, 143 m.p.h.; service ceiling, 24,000 ft.; range (12 passengers and 265 lb. baggage), 497 mls., (8 passengers and 150 lb. baggage), 1,225 mls., (3,000-lb. payload), 125 mls.
Weights: Empty, 4,615 lb.; max. loaded, 8,040 lb.
Accommodation: Pilot and 8–12 passengers, or five stretchers and five sitting casualties or attendants.
Status: In production. First of three prototypes flown February 23, 1966. Initial production batch of eight aircraft was scheduled to be completed by the beginning of 1968.
Notes: Capable of operation from skis and floats as well as the standard wheel undercarriage, the Skyservant places accent on versatility and simplicity of maintenance. Large double-doors are provided for freight loading, and the seats may be removed to provide 283 cu. ft. of unobstructed cargo space.

86

DORNIER SKYSERVANT

Dimensions: Span, 49 ft. 2½ in.; length, 37 ft. 4¾ in.; height, 12 ft. 9½ in.; wing area, 302 sq. ft.

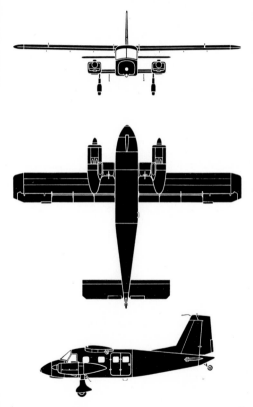

DORNIER DO 31E

Country of Origin: Federal Germany.
Type: Military V/STOL Tactical Transport.
Power Plants: Two Bristol Siddeley BS.53 Pegasus B.Pg.5–2 vectored-thrust turbofans each rated at 15,000 lb.s.t., and eight Rolls-Royce RB.162–4D lift turbojets each rated at 4,400 lb.s.t.
Performance: (Estimated) Maximum cruising speed, 452 m.p.h. at 30,000 ft. (Mach 0·67); normal cruising speed, 404 m.p.h. at 19,685 ft. (Mach 0·58); initial climb rate (Pegasus engines only), 3,780 ft./min.; service ceiling, 35,100 ft.; range (with maximum payload—11,020 lb.), 1,118 mls.; ferry range, 2,858 mls.
Weights: Loaded (VTOL), 49,500 lb.; maximum loaded, 60,500 lb.
Accommodation: Crew of two side-by-side with dual controls. Freight hold has volume of 1,766 cu. ft., and can accommodate 36 troops or 24 casualty stretchers.
Status: Experimental programme. First prototype was flown (without lift engines) on February 10, 1967, and second on July 15, 1967.
Notes: Do 31E1 used as conventional aircraft for testing airframe and cruise engines. Second flying prototype, the Do 31E3, has been tested with lift engines, thrust lines of lift engines being controllable 15° fore and aft by means of rotating nozzles. First vertical flight effected November 22, 1967.

DORNIER DO 31E

Dimensions: Span, 59 ft. 3 in.; length, 67 ft. 11 in.; height, 27 ft. 11¾ in.; wing area, 613·542 sq. ft.

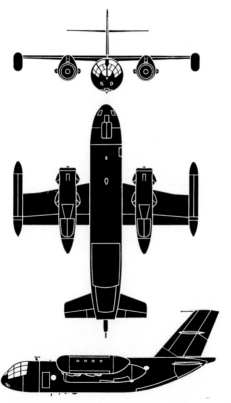

DOUGLAS DC-8 SUPER 60 SERIES

Country of Origin: U.S.A.

Type: Long-range Commercial Transport.

Power Plants: Four Pratt & Whitney JT3D-3B turbo-fans each rated at 18,000 lb.s.t., or (Super 63) JT3D-7 turbofans each rated at 19,000 lb.s.t.

Performance: (Variant indicated in parentheses) Maximum cruising speed at 220,000 lb., (61) 580 m.p.h., (62) 586 m.p.h., (63) 583 m.p.h.; initial climb rate at maximum loaded weight, (61) 2,270 ft./min., (62) 2,240 ft./min., (63) 2,165 ft./min.; maximum range without payload, (61) 7,370 mls., (62) 8,780 mls., (63) 8,100 mls.

Weights: Operational empty, (61) 150,298 lb., (62) 143,653 lb., (63) 156,755 lb.; maximum loaded, (61) 325,000 lb., (62) 335,000 lb., (63) 350,000 lb.

Accommodation: The maximum economy class passenger accommodation of the Super 60 series is as follows: (61) 251, (62) 189, (63) 251 plus 14,000 lb. freight. The space-limited payloads of the freighter equivalents are: (61F) 91,250 lb., (62F) 96,754 lb., (63F) 91,614 lb.

Status: In production. First DC-8-61 flown March 14, 1966, first DC-8-62 flown August 29, 1966 and first DC-8-63 flown April 10, 1967.

Notes: Stretched derivatives of DC-8-50 (see 1966 edition). DC-8-61 (illustrated above) and -61F feature 36·9-ft increase in fuselage length. DC-8-62 and -62F have shorter fuselage, 3-ft. wingtip extensions, new engine pylons suspending the engines 40 in. forward of previous installations, and redesigned long-duct engine pods offering reduced drag. The DC-8-63 (illustrated opposite) and -63F have similar fuselage to -61 coupled with aerodynamic refinements of -62 and more powerful engines.

90

DOUGLAS DC-8 SUPER 60 SERIES

Dimensions: Span (61), 142 ft. 4¾ in., (62 and 63) 148 ft. 4¾ in.; length (61 and 63), 187 ft. 4¾ in., (62) 157 ft. 4¾ in.; height, 42 ft. 3½ in.; wing area (61), 2,884 sq. ft., (62 and 63) 2,926·8 sq. ft.

DOUGLAS DC-9 SERIES 30

Country of Origin: U.S.A.

Type: Short- and Medium-range Commercial Transport.

Power Plants: Two Pratt & Whitney JT8D-7 turbofans each rated at 14,000 lb.s.t.

Performance: Maximum cruising speed, 565 m.p.h. at 25,000 ft.; range (with one hour and 230 mls. reserves), 1,484 mls. at 540 m.p.h. at 30,000 ft. (Mach 0·8), at long-range cruising speed at 30,000 ft., 1,725 mls.

Weights: Empty, 52,935 lb.; max. loaded, 98,000 lb.

Accommodation: Crew of two plus cabin attendants and up to 115 passengers.

Status: In production. DC-9-10 flown on February 25, 1965 with deliveries following in November 1965. DC-9-30 flown August 1, 1966, with deliveries commencing 1967, and DC-9-40 flown November 28, 1967 with deliveries scheduled for late spring 1968.

Notes: DC-9-30 differs from DC-9-10 (see 1966 edition) in having 14·9-ft. longer fuselage, 2-ft. wingtip extensions, full-span leading-edge slats, and JT8D-7 turbofans delivering full take-off thrust under all atmospheric temperatures up to 84° F. The smaller DC-9-10 series includes the Models 11 and 15, the former having JT8D-5 engines derated to 12,000 lb.s.t., and the latter having JT8D-1 engines of 14,000 lb.s.t. Current developments of the basic DC-9 design include the DC-9-40 with two 38-in. sections added to the fuselage, one forward and the other aft of the wings, and 14,500 lb.s.t. JT8D-9 turbofans, this version accommodating up to 125 passengers and maximum loaded weight of 108,000 lb. C-9A is U.S.A.F. aeromedical evacuation transport version of DC-9-10.

92

DOUGLAS DC-9 SERIES 30

Dimensions: Span, 93 ft. 4¾ in.; length, 119 ft. 3½ in.; height, 27 ft. 6 in.; wing area, 1,000·7 sq. ft.

DOUGLAS A-4F SKYHAWK

Country of Origin: U.S.A.

Type: Single-seat Shipboard Attack Bomber.

Power Plant: One Pratt & Whitney J52-P-8A turbojet rated at 9,300 lb.s.t.

Performance: Maximum speed (without external stores), 675 m.p.h. at sea level (Mach 0·88), 612 m.p.h. at 35,000 ft. (Mach 0·92); maximum speed in high drag configuration, 610 m.p.h. at sea level (Mach 0·8), 575 m.p.h. at 30,000 ft. (Mach 0·85); combat radius (with 4,000 lb. external stores), 380 mls.; ferry range (maximum external fuel), 2,440 mls.; service ceiling (clean), 47,900 ft.

Weights: Empty, 9,940 lb.; loaded (clean), 16,300 lb.; maximum loaded, 27,420 lb.

Armament: Two 20-mm. Mk. 12 cannon with 100 r.p.g. plus a maximum of 8,200 lb. of stores for shipboard and 11,800 lb. for shore-based operation.

Status: In production. First A-4F flown August 31, 1966, with deliveries of 150 to U.S. Navy initiated June 20, 1967.

Notes: A-4F differs from A-4E in having more powerful engine, steerable nosewheel, zero-zero escape system, avionics compartment aft of cockpit and wing, lift spoilers. Tandem two-seat training version, the TA-4F, also being manufactured with 139 on order. A-4G and TA-4G equivalent versions for Australian Navy.

94

DOUGLAS A-4F SKYHAWK

Dimensions: Span, 27 ft. 6 in.; length, 42 ft. 10¾ in.; height, 15 ft. 2 in.; wing area, 260 sq. ft.

FAIRCHILD HILLER FH-227B

Country of Origin: U.S.A.

Type: Short- and Medium-range Commercial Transport.

Power Plants: Two Rolls-Royce Dart Mk. 532–7 turboprops each rated at 2,250 e.s.h.p.

Performance: Maximum speed, 300 m.p.h.; maximum cruising speed, 288 m.p.h. at 5,500–9,000 ft.; economical cruising speed, 276 m.p.h. at 25,000 ft.; maximum range (with 8,400-lb. payload and 45 min. reserves), 1,610 mls. at 25,000 ft., (with maximum payload—13,490 lb.), 440 mls.

Weights: Operational empty, 27,510 lb.; maximum loaded, 45,500 lb.

Accommodation: Crew comprises pilot, co-pilot and stewardess, and accommodation is provided in standard configuration for 44 passengers, with alternative high-density cabin configuration for 56 passengers.

Status: In production. First FH-227 completed February 2, 1966. First delivery of FH-227B (to Piedmont) December 1966.

Notes: The FH-227B is the current production version of the stretched derivative of the licence-built Fokker F.27 Friendship (see pages 102–3). The FH-227 embodies a 6·5 ft. increase in overall fuselage length, the FH-227B featuring some structural strengthening, new wheels, brakes, and larger (12·5-ft. diameter) airscrews.

96

FAIRCHILD HILLER FH-227B

Dimensions: Span, 95 ft. 2 in.; length, 83 ft. 8 in.; height, 27 ft. 6 in.; wing area, 754 sq. ft.

FAIRCHILD HILLER F-228

Country of Origin: U.S.A.

Type: Short-haul Commercial Transport.

Power Plants: Two Rolls-Royce RB.203-01 Trent turbofans each rated at 9,730 lb.s.t.

Performance: (Estimated) Maximum cruising speed, 495 m.p.h. at 20,000 ft.; economical cruising speed, 368 m.p.h. at 20,000 ft.; initial climb rate, 2,970 ft./min.; service ceiling, 35,000 ft.; range (with maximum payload—8,500 lb.), 540 mls. at economical cruising speed.

Weights: Maximum loaded, 54,500 lb.

Accommodation: Normal flight crew of two and alternative arrangements for 50 or 55 passengers in five-abreast seating, or for 60 passengers in maximum high-density seating arrangement.

Status: In production. First F-228 scheduled to fly late autumn 1968, first deliveries following early 1970.

Notes: The F-228 is a derivative of the Fokker F.28 Fellowship (see pages 104–5) and incorporating a shortened version of the F.28 fuselage, part of the F.28 wing structure, and the F.28 tail assembly, approximately half the airframe being manufactured by Fairchild Hiller and the remainder by Fokker, HFB, VFW and Short Brothers. Fairchild Hiller has ordered 50 sets of components, deliveries of these having commenced late 1967. The F-228 is intended primarily for the regional airline short-haul market but may be used also as a corporate executive aircraft.

FAIRCHILD HILLER F-228

Dimensions: Span, 78 ft. 9 in.; length, 86 ft. 8 in.; height, 27 ft. 8 in.; wing area, 822 sq. ft.

FIAT G.91Y

Country of Origin: Italy.
Type: Single-seat Strike and Reconnaissance Fighter.
Power Plant: Two General Electric J85-GE-13A turbo-jets each rated at 2,725 lb.s.t. and 4,080 lb.s.t. with afterburning.
Performance: (Estimated) Maximum speed, 714 m.p.h. at sea level (Mach 0·94), 690 m.p.h. at 32,810 ft. (Mach 0·975); climb to 19,685 ft., 1·5 min., to 29,530 ft., 2·3 min.; service ceiling, 49,200 ft.; ferry range, 1,926 mls.
Weights: Empty, 8,378 lb.; normal loaded, 17,196 lb.; maximum loaded, 19,180 lb.
Armament: Four 0·5-in. Colt-Browning machine guns and four 500-lb. bombs, twelve 3-in. HVAR rockets, or two Nord AS.20 or AS.30L ASMs.
Status: Under development. First of two prototypes flown December 27, 1966. An initial series of 20 ordered for evaluation.
Notes: Although bearing a close resemblance to the Fiat G.91R (see 1966 edition), the G.91Y possesses little commonality with its predecessor which it is intended to replace in Italian Air Force service. While the basic concept remains unchanged, the G.91Y possesses appreciably more power and offers substantially improved load-carrying capability. Like the G.91R, the G.91Y is intended to operate from semi-prepared strips, and a tandem two-seat trainer version, the G.91YT, is currently proposed. It is anticipated that the G.91Y will enter service in 1969–70.

FIAT G.91Y

Dimensions: Span, 29 ft. 6½ in.; length, 38 ft. 3½ in.; height, 14 ft. 6⅓ in.; wing area, 195·149 sq. ft.

FOKKER F.27 FRIENDSHIP SRS. 200

Country of Origin: Netherlands.

Type: Short-haul Commercial Transport.

Power Plants: Two Rolls-Royce Dart 532-7 turboprops each rated at 2,250 e.s.h.p.

Performance: Maximum cruising speed, 330 m.p.h. at 20,000 ft.; economical cruising speed (at 38,000 lb.), 295 m.p.h. at 20,000 ft.; initial climb rate, 1,350 ft./min.; service ceiling, 28,500 ft.; range (maximum fuel and 10,266-lb. payload), 1,285 mls.

Weights: Empty (48-seat version), 23,204 lb.; maximum loaded, 43,500 lb.

Accommodation: Basic flight crew of two or three and standard accommodation for 40 passengers with alternative layout for up to 52 passengers.

Status: In production. Total of 275 ordered from Fokker by November 1, 1967, plus 183 from Fairchild Hiller.

Notes: In continuous production for 10 years. Initial production version, the Srs. 100, powered by 1,850 e.s.h.p. Dart 514-7s and licence-built by Fairchild Hiller as F-27. The Srs. 200, described above and illustrated, produced by Fairchild Hiller as F-27A, and the Srs. 300, which is similar to the Srs. 100 apart from reinforced floor and large cargo door, as F-27B. Srs. 400 is equivalent version of Srs. 200.

102

FOKKER F-27 FRIENDSHIP SRS. 200

Dimensions: Span, 95 ft. 2 in.; length, 77 ft. 1½ in.; height, 27 ft. 11 in.; wing area, 754 sq. ft.

FOKKER F.28 FELLOWSHIP

Country of Origin: Netherlands.
Type: Short-haul Commercial Transport.
Power Plants: Two Rolls-Royce RB.183-2 Mk. 555-15
Spey Junior turbofans each rated at 9,850 lb.s.t.
Performance: Maximum cruising speed, 527 m.p.h. at
21,000 ft.; economical cruising speed, 519 m.p.h. at
25,000 ft.; long-range cruising speed, 426 m.p.h.;
range (with 60 passengers), 627 mls., (with maximum
fuel), 1,200 mls.
Weights: Operational empty, 33,090 lb.; maximum
loaded, 56,700 lb.
Accommodation: Alternative arrangements for 40 passengers in first-class seating four abreast, or 55, 60
or 65 passengers in five-abreast all-tourist seating.
Status: In production. First prototype flown May 9,
1967, followed by second prototype on August 3, 1967.
First production deliveries (to Braathens S.A.F.E.)
scheduled to commence at the end of 1968.
Notes: The F.28 Fellowship is a European co-opera-
tive effort in which the nose section is of Fokker
design and production; fuselage section 1 is of Fokker
design and VFW construction; fuselage sections 2
and 3 are of Fokker design and production; wing
centre section is of Fokker design and production;
outer wing is of Short Brothers design and production;
fuselage section 4 and engine nacelles are of HFB
design and construction, and the tail assembly is of
VFW design and construction.

FOKKER F.28 FELLOWSHIP

Dimensions: Span, 77 ft. 4¼ in.; length, 89 ft. 10¾ in.; height, 27 ft. 9½ in.; wing area, 822 sq. ft.

FOUND MODEL 100 CENTENNIAL

Country of Origin: Canada.

Type: Light Utility Aircraft.

Power Plant: One Lycoming IO-540-G six-cylinder horizontally-opposed engine rated at 290 h.p.

Performance: (Estimated) Maximum speed, 160 m.p.h. at sea level; cruising speed (75% power), 150 m.p.h., (65% power), 140 m.p.h.; initial climb rate, 1,125 ft./min.; service ceiling, 20,000 ft.; range, (65% power), 700 mls.

Weights: Empty, 1,750 lb.; loaded, 3,500 lb.

Accommodation: Cabin may be equipped for a maximum of six persons, and as an ambulance two casualty stretchers and a medical attendant may be accommodated.

Status: In production. Prototype flown April 8, 1967. First production aircraft delivered October 1967 when production rate was two per month with a planned rate of four per month from beginning of 1968.

Notes: The Centennial has been designed specifically for operation in undeveloped areas, and is suitable for use as a light freighter, aerial survey, or agricultural aircraft. The cabin has a volume of 130 cu. ft. and an unobstructed floor, and large freight-loading doors are provided in both sides of the fuselage.

FOUND MODEL 100 CENTENNIAL

Dimensions: Span, 39 ft. 0 in.; length, 26 ft. 6 in.;
height, 8 ft. 4 in.; wing area, 196·6 sq. ft.

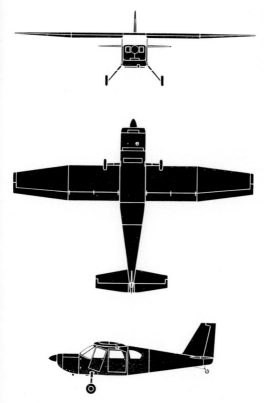

GENERAL DYNAMICS F-111A

Country of Origin: U.S.A.

Type: Two-seat Tactical Strike and Reconnaissance Fighter.

Power Plants: Two Pratt & Whitney TF30-P-3 turbofans each rated at approx. 12,500 lb.s.t. and 21,000 lb.s.t. with afterburning.

Performance: Maximum speed, 1,650 m.p.h. at 40,000 ft. (Mach 2·5), 865 m.p.h. at sea level (Mach 1·2); service ceiling (without external stores), 55,000–60,000 ft., (with maximum conventional bomb load), 30,000–35,000 ft.; tactical radius (hi-lo-hi mission with 16,000-lb. combat load), 1,500–1,700 mls.; ferry range, 3,500–4,000 mls.

Weights: Normal loaded, 81,400 lb.

Armament: One 20-mm. General Electric M-61A1 rotary cannon with 2,000 rounds, and ordnance loads such as 12 750-lb. M.117 bombs on triple ejector racks attached to four swivelling inboard pylons.

Status: In production. First deliveries against contracts for 331 F-111As for U.S.A.F. effected October 1967.

Notes: Variants of basic F-111 design include shipboard F-111B (see 1966 edition) of which 24 ordered; the F-111C for the R.A.A.F. with extended wing and strengthened undercarriage of the FB-111 (see pages 110–11), and the F-111K externally similar to the F-111C but possessing later avionics. Fifty F-111Ks are on order for the R.A.F.

GENERAL DYNAMICS F-111A

Dimensions: Span, 63 ft. 0 in., (maximum sweep), 31 ft. 11 in.; length, 73 ft. 6 in.; height, 17 ft. 1½ in.

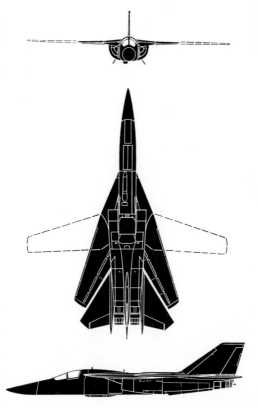

GENERAL DYNAMICS FB-111A

Country of Origin: U.S.A.
Type: Two-seat Strategic Bomber.
Power Plants: Two Pratt & Whitney TF30-P-3 turbo-fans each rated at approx. 12,500 lb.s.t. and 21,000 lb.s.t. with afterburning.
Performance: (Estimated) Maximum speed (without external stores), 1,450 m.p.h. at 40,000 ft. (Mach 2·2), 838 m.p.h. at sea level (Mach 1·1); normal combat radius, 1,250 mls.; maximum ferry range, 4,100 mls.
Weights: Maximum loaded, 110,000 lb.
Armament: Four SRAM (Short-range Attack Missiles) or conventional ordnance loads up to maximum of 36,000 lb. (e.g. 48 750-lb. bombs on multiple ejection racks on four swivelling and four fixed pylons).
Status: In production. Prototype flown July 30, 1967. Initial orders for 64 with deliveries to U.S.A.F. Strategic Air Command commencing 1968. Total of 210 FB-111A bombers programmed.
Notes: An interim strategic bomber derivative of the F-111A tactical strike and reconnaissance fighter (see pages 108–9), the FB-111A features an extended wing, a strengthened undercarriage with increased braking capacity to cater for higher take-off and landing weights, and Mk. 2B advanced avionics for improved navigation and air-to-ground weapons delivery. The non-swivelling outer pylons are intended for subsonic flight and are jettisoned when wing sweep exceeds 26° for supersonic flight. The U.S.A.F. is to establish seven main bases for the Strategic Air Command's FB-111A bomber force.

GENERAL DYNAMICS FB-111A

Dimensions: Span, 70 ft. 0 in., (maximum sweep), 33 ft. 11 in.; length, 73 ft. 6 in.; height, 17 ft. 0 in.

GRUMMAN A-6A INTRUDER

Country of Origin: U.S.A.
Type: Two-seat Shipboard Low-level Strike Aircraft.
Power Plants: Two Pratt & Whitney J52-P-8A turbojets each rated at 9,300 lb.s.t.
Performance: Maximum speed, 685 m.p.h. at sea level (Mach 0·9), 625 m.p.h. at 36,000 ft. (Mach 0·95); normal cruising speed, 480 m.p.h. at 28,000 ft.; low-level long-range cruising speed (high drag configuration), 345 m.p.h.; range at low-altitude (internal fuel only), 1,250 mls., (with five 250 Imp. gal./300 U.S. gal. drop tanks), 1,950 mls.; ferry range, 3,225 mls. at 28,000 ft.
Weights: Empty, 25,684 lb.; loaded (maximum internal fuel), 43,000 lb.; maximum overload, 60,626 lb.
Armament: Maximum offensive load for limited-range interdiction is 15,000 lb. distributed on five 3,600-lb. capacity pylons. Typical conventional loads include eighteen 500-lb. Mk. 82 bombs plus two 250 Imp. gal./300 U.S. gal. tanks, five 1,000-lb. Mk. 83 or 2,000-lb. Mk. 84 bombs, or four AGM-12 Bullpup ASMs.
Status: In production. First of eight test and evaluation aircraft flown April 19, 1960. Deliveries to U.S. Navy commenced in 1963.
Notes: A-6A currently serves with both U.S. Navy and U.S. Marine Corps. Simplified A-6B version with DIANE (Digital Integrated Attack Navigation) system deleted was cancelled in favour of A-7A Corsair II.

112

GRUMMAN A-6A INTRUDER

Dimensions: Span, 53 ft. 0 in.; length, 54 ft. 7 in.;
height, 15 ft. 7 in.; wing area, 529 sq. ft.

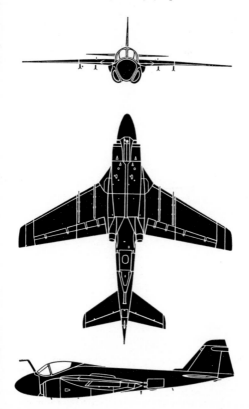

H

GRUMMAN C-2A GREYHOUND

Country of Origin: U.S.A.
Type: Carrier On-board Delivery Transport.
Power Plants: Two Allison T56-A-8A turboprops each rated at 4,050 e.s.h.p.
Performance: Maximum speed, 329 m.p.h. at 11,300 ft.; average cruising speed, 306 m.p.h. at 27,300 ft.; initial climb rate (at 54,812 lb.), 2,090 ft./min.; range (with 10,000-lb. payload), 1,520 mls.; ferry range, 1,998 mls.; service ceiling, 34,300 ft.
Weights: Empty, 31,154 lb.; loaded, 54,830 lb.
Accommodation: Normal crew comprises pilot and co-pilot. The fully pressurised cargo compartment can accommodate up to 15,000 lb. cargo on either three master pallets or five modular pallets, and alternative loads include 39 troops, or 20 casualty stretchers.
Status: In production. First aircraft flown on November 18, 1964, and deliveries of seventeen to U.S. Fleet commenced in 1966.
Notes: Evolved specifically for the transportation of freight and personnel between land bases and carriers at sea, and compatible with the elevators and hangar decks of the U.S. Navy's CVS-10, CVA-19 and larger carriers, the C-2A Greyhound is a derivative of the E-2A Hawkeye (see pages 116-17), employing a virtually identical wing and similar main undercarriage members, cockpit, power plants and tail surfaces. Provision is made for carrying two 250 Imp. gal./300 U.S. gal. or 375 Imp. gal./450 U.S. gal. external fuel tanks on sides of fuselage, or buddy refuelling packs.

GRUMMAN C-2A GREYHOUND

Dimensions: Span, 80 ft. 7 in.; length 56 ft. 6 in.;
height, 15 ft. 11 in.; wing area, 700 sq. ft.

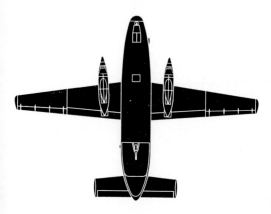

GRUMMAN E-2A HAWKEYE

Country of Origin: U.S.A.
Type: Shipboard Early Warning, Surface Surveillance and Strike Control Aircraft.
Power Plants: Two Allison T56-A-8A turboprops each rated at 4,050 e.s.h.p.
Performance: Maximum speed, 397 m.p.h. at sea level; cruising speed, 316 m.p.h.; initial climb rate, 4,200 ft./min.; normal operational altitude (for surface surveillance and strike control tasks), 25,000 ft., (for early warning task), 30,000 ft.; normal endurance on station, 5 hr.; maximum endurance on station, 7 hr.
Weights: Empty, 36,063 lb.; loaded, 49,638 lb.
Accommodation: Crew comprises pilot and co-pilot, an avionics technician, a combat intelligence centre officer and an air control officer. The three controllers are seated side-by-side to port in the ATDS (Airborne Tactical Data System) compartment.
Status: In production. First prototype flown on October 21, 1960, and first fully-equipped prototype flew on April 19, 1961. Production deliveries commenced January 19, 1964.
Notes: Designed for early warning protection of fleet units, the E-2A is currently used to monitor and control U.S. Navy air strikes over North Vietnam.

GRUMMAN E-2A HAWKEYE

Dimensions: Span, 80 ft. 7 in.; length, 56 ft. 3½ in.; height, 16 ft. 4¾ in.; wing area, 700 sq. ft.

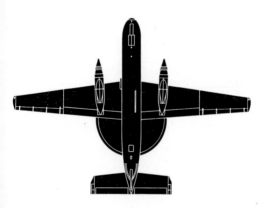

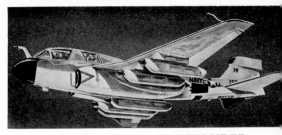

GRUMMAN EA-6B INTRUDER

Country of Origin: U.S.A.

Type: Four-seat All-weather Shipboard Electronic Countermeasures Aircraft.

Power Plants: Two Pratt & Whitney J52-P-8A turbojets each rated at 9,300 lb.s.t.

Performance: (Estimated) Maximum speed, 670 m.p.h. at sea level, 610 m.p.h. at 36,000 ft.; low-level long-range cruising speed (high drag configuration), 345 m.p.h.; low-altitude range (internal fuel), 1,250 mls.

Weights: Empty, 34,581 lb.; maximum loaded, 58,500 lb.

Status: Prototype development. First prototype scheduled to fly early 1968.

Notes: The EA-6B is a four-seat development of the two-seat EA-6A electronic countermeasures aircraft, retaining the basic aerodynamic design, power plant installation and associated subsystems. The principal change is in the forward fuselage which has been extended by 40 in. in order to allow for the insertion of an additional cockpit accommodating two extra crew members in side-by-side seats, these operating the advanced avionics system, much of which is accommodated in pods beneath the wings and fuselage. These pods contain their own generators which are driven by small airscrews attached to the pods themselves. The EA-6B has sensors which detect, locate, classify and jam enemy radiation.

118

GRUMMAN EA-6B INTRUDER

Dimensions: Span, 53 ft. 0 in.; length, 59 ft. 5 in.; height, 16 ft. 3 in.; wing area, 529 sq. ft.

GRUMMAN G-1159 GULFSTREAM II

Country of Origin: U.S.A.

Type: Corporate Executive Transport.

Power Plants: Two Rolls-Royce RB.163-25 Spey Mk. 511-8 turbofans each rated at 11,400 lb.s.t.

Performance: Maximum speed, 585 m.p.h.; maximum cruising speed (at 45,000 lb.), 561 m.p.h. at 40,000 ft.; long-range cruising speed, 496 m.p.h. at 43,000 ft.; time to 40,000 ft. (at 56,000 lb.), 14·5 min.; range (including allowances for 200-mile diversion plus 30 min. fuel), 3,680 mls.

Weights: Empty, 28,116 lb.; max. loaded, 56,000 lb.

Accommodation: Normal crew of three and various cabin arrangements for 10–19 passengers.

Status: In production. First prototype flown on October 2, 1966. Initial production deliveries were scheduled to commence late 1967 with production rate of three per month being attained by late 1968. More than 70 Gulfstream IIs had been ordered by November 1967, taking production through 1969.

Notes: Optimised for the corporate executive transport role, the Gulfstream II embodies much experience gained with the manufacture of more than 190 G-159 Gulfstream I turboprop-powered executive transports, the earlier type still being manufactured at a rate of one per month during 1966. The Gulfstream II has an interior size virtually identical to that of the Gulfstream I and comparable take-off performance, coupled with transcontinental range and substantial increase in performance.

GRUMMAN G-1159 GULFSTREAM II

Dimensions: Span, 68 ft. 10 in.; length, 79 ft. 11 in.; height, 24 ft. 6 in.; wing area, 793·5 sq. ft.

GRUMMAN TC-4C

Country of Origin: U.S.A.

Type: Attack Crew Proficiency Trainer.

Power Plants: Two Rolls-Royce Dart Mk. 529-8X turboprops each rated at 2,210 e.s.h.p.

Performance: Maximum speed, 386 m.p.h.; maximum cruising speed, 334 m.p.h.; service ceiling, 30,400 ft.; ferry range, 2,245 mls.

Weights: Empty, 24,575 lb.; max. loaded, 36,000 lb.

Accommodation: Flight crew of two, two instructors, one pupil pilot and four bombardier-navigator pupils.

Status: In production. First of nine flown June 14, 1967 with deliveries scheduled for completion March 1968. First to U.S. Navy scheduled for early 1968.

Notes: The TC-4C is a derivative of the commercial Gulfstream I intended to improve the proficiency of A-6A Intruder crews through realistic in-flight training with actual A-6A avionics. The TC-4C is a standard Gulfstream I airframe mated to an actual A-6A radome containing standard search and track radar installations. Simulated A-6A missions may be flown by a pilot-bombardier/navigator team in a full-scale A-6A cockpit situated in the aft portion of the TC-4C.

GRUMMAN TC-4C

Dimensions: Span, 78 ft. 4 in.; length, 67 ft. 11 in.; height, 22 ft. 9 in.; wing area, 610 sq. ft.

HANDLEY PAGE HERALD SERIES 200

Country of Origin: United Kingdom.
Type: Short- and Medium-haul Commercial Transport.
Power Plants: Two Rolls-Royce Dart Mk. 527 turbo-props each rated at 1,910 s.h.p. (2,105 e.s.h.p.).
Performance: Maximum cruising speed (at 39,500 lb.), 275 m.p.h. at 15,000 ft.; long-range cruising speed, 265 m.p.h. at 23,000 ft.; initial climb rate (at 41,000 lb.), 1,805 ft./min.; service ceiling (at 35,000 lb.), 27,900 ft.; range (with maximum fuel and no allowances), 1,760 mls., (with maximum payload—11,242 lb., 100-mile diversion and 45 min. holding), 700 mls.
Weights: Empty equipped, 24,400 lb.; maximum loaded, 43,000 lb.
Accommodation: Normal crew of two and alternative cabin arrangements for 50 or 56 passengers.
Status: In production. Prototype flown March 11, 1958, and first production aircraft October 30, 1959. Orders placed at time of closing for press called for Srs. 100, 36 Srs. 200, 83 Srs. 400 and 11 Srs. 700.
Notes: No decision has yet been taken to go ahead with the more powerful and heavier Herald Series 700 owing to the VASP order for 10 aircraft of this type having encountered considerable financial difficulties. The Herald Series 400 is a side-loading military transport derivative of the Series 200, accommodating 50 troops or 24 casualty stretchers, and incorporating a strengthened freight floor. The Herald Series 400 currently serves with the Royal Malaysian Air Force.

HANDLEY PAGE HERALD SERIES 200

Dimensions: Span, 94 ft. 9 in.; length, 75 ft. 6 in.; height, 24 ft. 1 in.; wing area, 886 sq. ft.

HANDLEY PAGE HP.137 JETSTREAM

Country of Origin: United Kingdom.
Type: Light Executive Transport and Feederliner.
Power Plants: Two Turboméca Astazou XIVC turbo-props each rated at 850 e.s.h.p.
Performance: Maximum cruising speed, 300 m.p.h. at 15,000 ft.; economical cruising speed, 240 m.p.h. at 30,000 ft.; range (maximum fuel), 2,205 mls., (18 passengers), 345 mls.
Weights: Basic operational, 8,500 lb.; maximum loaded, 12,500 lb.
Accommodation: Flight crew of two and maximum of 18 passengers in high-density feederliner configuration. Alternative interior arrangements for 8–12 passengers in corporate executive version.
Status: In production. First of three prototypes flown August 18, 1967. First production Jetstream scheduled to be completed March 1968, current plans calling for the completion of 44 aircraft by the end of 1968, a production peak of 10 per month being attained by mid-1969.
Notes: Offered with eight standard interiors accommodating from eight to 18 passengers, the Jetstream is intended to fulfil corporate executive, feederline and air taxi requirements, and is to be sold primarily through distributors, 65 having been ordered by International Jetstream Corporation and 100 having been ordered by C.S.E. Aviation. It was anticipated that certification would be obtained by February 1968.

HANDLEY PAGE HP.137 JETSTREAM

Dimensions: Span, 52 ft. 0 in.; length, 47 ft. 1½ in.; height, 17 ft. 5½ in.; wing area, 270 sq. ft.

HANDLEY PAGE VICTOR B.(S.R.) MK. 2

Country of Origin: United Kingdom.
Type: Long-range Strategic Reconnaissance and Surveillance Aircraft.
Power Plants: Four Rolls-Royce Conway R.Co.17 Mk. 201 turbofans each rated at 19,750 lb.s.t.
Performance: (Estimated) Maximum speed, 630 m.p.h. at 36,000–50,000 ft. (Mach 0·95); maximum cruising speed, 610 m.p.h. at 55,000 ft.; long-range cruising speed, 560 m.p.h. at 40,000 ft. (Mach 0·85); radius of action (high-altitude mission), 2,300–2,500 mls.; maximum range (with underwing and weapons bay tanks), 5,500–6,000 mls.
Weight: Maximum loaded, 200,000 lb.
Accommodation: Crew of five in pressurised nose compartment. Camera equipment housed in packs mounted in the weapons bay, these packs accommodating a wide variety of camera combinations for day and night reconnaissance and aerial survey. In addition to a camera pack, the weapons bay can house three canisters containing a total of 108 photoflashes, or two photoflash canisters and an auxiliary fuel tank. Alternatively, a camera pack and two auxiliary tanks may be carried.
Status: Production completed but conversion of B. Mk. 2s to B.(S.R.) Mk. 2s continuing late 1967.
Note: The B.(S.R.) Mk. 2 is essentially similar to the B. Mk. 2 (see 1966 edition) and can be reconverted for the bombing role. One S.R. Mk. 2 is capable of radar-mapping the entire Mediterranean in one seven-hour sortie.

HANDLEY PAGE VICTOR B.(S.R.) MK. 2

Dimensions: Span, 120 ft. 0 in.; length, 114 ft. 11 in.; height, 30 ft. 1½ in.; wing area, 2,597 sq. ft.

HAWKER SIDDELEY HS.125 SERIES 3AR

Country of Origin: United Kingdom.

Type: Light Executive Transport.

Power Plants: Two Bristol Siddeley Viper 522 turbojets each rated at 3,360 lb.s.t.

Performance: Maximum cruising speed, 507 m.p.h. at 30,000 ft.; long-range cruising speed, 429 m.p.h. at 40,000 ft.; range with maximum fuel and 1,700-lb. payload, 1,340 mls. at maximum cruising speed, 1,800 mls. at long-range cruising speed (with 45 min. reserves); time to 35,000 ft., 16·5 min.

Weights: Empty, 12,000 lb.; maximum loaded, 22,700 lb.

Accommodation: Normal seating for two crew members and six passengers but high-density seating arrangement available for maximum of 10 passengers.

Status: In production. First HS.125 flown August 13, 1962, followed by first production model on February 12, 1963. Current production rate of three per month with approximately 125 scheduled for delivery by the beginning of 1968.

Notes: The HS.125 Series 3AR is a longer-range version of the Series 3A with an additional 112 Imp. gal. of fuel in a faired ventral tank which reduces drag and increases maximum cruise Mach number at 30,000 ft. from 0·737 to 0·752. The Series 3AR, which was undergoing trials during the autumn and winter of 1967, also features wheel-well closure doors and a higher gross weight, and a ventral fin has been introduced. A navigational training version of the HS.125 for the R.A.F. is the Series 2 Dominie T. Mk. 1 (see 1966 edition) which serves with No. 1 Air Navigation School.

HAWKER SIDDELEY HS.125 SERIES 3AR

Dimensions: Span, 47 ft. 0 in.; length, 47 ft. 5 in.; height, 16 ft. 6 in.; wing area, 353 sq. ft.

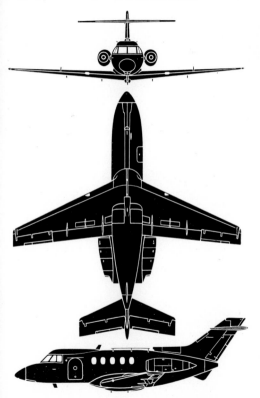

HAWKER SIDDELEY 748 SERIES 2

Country of Origin: United Kingdom.
Type: Short- and Medium-Range Commercial Transport.
Power Plants: Two Rolls-Royce Dart R.Da.7 Mk. 531 turboprops each rated at 2,105 e.s.h.p.
Performance: Maximum speed, 312 m.p.h. at 16,000 ft.; maximum cruising speed, 274 m.p.h. at 10,000 ft.; economical cruising speed, 267 m.p.h. at 20,000 ft.; range cruising speed, 259 m.p.h. at 25,000 ft.; initial climb rate, 1,150 ft./min.; range (with max. fuel and 9,785-lb. payload), 1,577 mls. at 230 m.p.h. at 19,500 ft.
Weights: Empty, 24,572 lb.; basic operational, 25,590 lb.; maximum loaded, 44,495 lb.
Accommodation: Crew of two plus cabin attendants, and alternative cabin arrangements for 40 or 48 passengers. High-density arrangement for 62 passengers.
Status: In production. First prototype flown June 24, 1960. First production aircraft (Srs. 1) flown August 30, 1961. Eighteen Srs. 1 aircraft delivered, plus four assembled in India by HAL for Indian Air Force. HAL is also producing 32 Srs. 2 aircraft. Approximately 100 delivered by end of 1967 when production rate was three aircraft per month.

132

HAWKER SIDDELEY 748 SERIES 2

Dimensions: Span, 98 ft. 6 in.; length, 67 ft. 0 in.; height, 24 ft. 10 in.; wing area, 811 sq. ft.

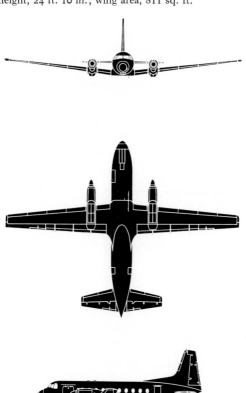

HAWKER SIDDELEY ANDOVER C. MK. 1

Country of Origin: United Kingdom.
Type: Military Tactical Transport.
Power Plants: Two Rolls-Royce Dart R.Da.12 Mk. 210C turboprops each rated at 2,970 s.h.p.
Performance: Maximum speed, 302 m.p.h. at 15,000 ft.; normal cruising speed (at 45,000 lb.), 258 m.p.h. at 20,000 ft.; initial climb rate, 1,170 ft./min.; service ceiling, 24,000 ft.; range (with maximum payload—14,750 lb.), 374 mls., (10,000-lb. payload), 1,186 mls.
Weights: Empty, 26,615 lb.; basic operational, 27,914 lb.; maximum loaded, 50,000 lb.
Accommodation: Flight crew of two or three, and 44 troops, 30 paratroops or 18 casualty stretchers, five sitting casualties and three medical attendants. A 10,500-lb. vehicle may be loaded over the ramp, and 1,200 lb. freight may be carried in flight on the ramp itself.
Status: Production complete. First Andover C. Mk. 1 flown on July 9, 1965, and last of 31 transports of this type flown by end of 1967.
Notes: Evolved from HS.748 (see pages 132–3), the Andover rear-loading transport utilises, with relatively minor modifications, the same forward fuselage and wing. The Andover C. Mk. 1 serves with Nos. 46 and 52 squadrons of R.A.F. Air Support Command.

HAWKER SIDDELEY ANDOVER C. MK. 1

Dimensions: Span, 98 ft. 3 in.; length, 77 ft. 11 in.; height, 30 ft. 1 in.; wing area, 831 sq. ft.

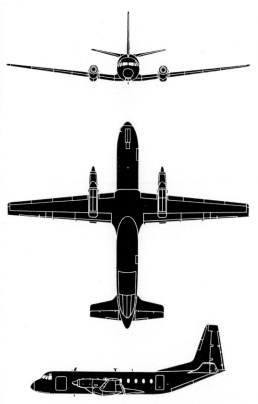

HAWKER SIDDELEY BUCCANEER S. MK. 2

Country of Origin: United Kingdom.

Type: Two-seat Shipboard Low-level Strike Aircraft.

Power Plants: Two Rolls-Royce RB.168-1 Spey R.Sp.2 Mk.101 turbofans each rated at 11,030 lb.s.t.

Performance: (Estimated) Maximum speed, 700 m.p.h. at sea level (Mach 0·92); maximum low-level cruising speed, 665 m.p.h. at 5,000 ft. (Mach 0·9); long-range cruising speed, 575 m.p.h. at 33,000 ft. (Mach 0·83); tactical radius (without external fuel), 500–600 mls. for hi-lo-lo-hi mission; ferry range (with two 250 Imp. gal./300 U.S. gal. underwing tanks and 750 Imp. gal./ 900 U.S. gal. weapons-bay tank), 1,800–2,000 mls.

Weights: Loaded (clean and without weapons), 42,000 lb.; maximum 54,000 lb.

Armament: Four 1,000-lb. bombs or large single store in weapons bay, and additional offensive stores on four 1,000-lb. capacity underwing pylons. These pylons may each carry a 1,000-lb. or 500-lb. bomb, 2-in. or 3-in. Glow worm rocket pack, 36-cell MATRA rocket dispenser, or AGM-12B Bullpup-A ASM.

Status: In production. First of two Spey-powered pre-production aircraft flown May 17, 1963. First production S. Mk. 2 flown June 5, 1964.

Notes: Reconnaissance pack housing six cameras may be mounted in weapons bay, with Lepus photoflood flares on wing pylons.

136

HAWKER SIDDELEY BUCCANEER S. MK. 2

Dimensions: Span, 42 ft. 4 in.; length, 63 ft. 5 in.;
height, 16 ft. 6 in.; wing area, 508·5 sq. ft.

HAWKER SIDDELEY HARRIER G.R. MK. 1

Country of Origin: United Kingdom.
Type: Single-seat V/STOL Ground Attack Fighter.
Power Plant: One Bristol Siddeley Pegasus 101 vectored-thrust turbofan rated at 19,000 lb.s.t.
Performance: (Estimated) Maximum speed, 660–680 m.p.h. at sea level; maximum cruising speed, 456 m.p.h. at sea level; initial climb rate, 35,000+ ft./min.; radius of action, 600 mls.; ferry range, 2,300 mls.
Weights: (Estimated) Empty, 12,000 lb.; Maximum loaded (VTOL), 15,000–16,000 lb., (STOL) 22,000 lb.
Armament: Up to 4,000 lb. external ordnance. Typical external load for short-range interdiction comprises six MATRA 18-rocket pods and a 1,000-lb. general-purpose bomb, plus two 30-mm. Aden cannon.
Status: In production. First of six pre-production Harriers flown August 31, 1966, and first aircraft against initial production quantity of 60 was scheduled to be completed before end of 1967. The Harrier G.R. Mk. 1 is scheduled to be cleared for delivery to R.A.F. by October 1968.
Notes: Evolved from the P.1127 and Kestrel, the Harrier will supplant the Hunter in R.A.F. service during 1969–70, and is intended to operate from the FEBA (Forward Edge of the Battle Area) to provide immediate close offensive support and reconnaissance. The Harrier is capable of being flown up to Mach 1·2 in a dive, and possesses reconnaissance capability, the single built-in side-looking camera being supplemented by ventral reconnaissance pod. A two-seat training version is under development.
138

HAWKER SIDDELEY HARRIER G.R. MK. 1

Dimensions: Span, 25 ft. 3 in.; length, 46 ft. 4 in.; height, 10 ft. 9 in.; wing area, 201 sq. ft.

HAWKER SIDDELEY NIMROD M.R. MK. I

Country of Origin: United Kingdom.
Type: Long-range Maritime Patrol Aircraft.
Power Plants: Four Rolls-Royce Spey Mk. 250 turbo-fans each rated at (approx.) 11,500 lb.s.t.
Performance: (Estimated) Maximum cruising speed, 500–530 m.p.h. at 31,000–33,000 ft.; long-range cruising speed, 450–460 m.p.h. at 30,000–35,000 ft.; loiter endurance (on two engines), 12–14 hr.
Weights: Maximum loaded, 160,000–170,000 lb.
Armament: Homing torpedoes, depth bombs, etc. in ventral weapons bay, and ASMs on wing pylons.
Accommodation: Normal crew complement of 11 members and (for emergency operation in transport role) some 60 fully-equipped troops.
Status: In production. First prototype flown May 23, 1967, and second prototype July 31, 1967. First of 38 production aircraft scheduled to fly during first quarter of 1968. First service deliveries scheduled for early 1969.
Notes: The Nimrod employs the basic structure of the Comet 4C transport, the principal change being the addition of an unpressurised pannier to accommodate the weapons bay and permit the retention of the Comet fuselage shell with its known pressurisation characteristics. The pressurised shell has been reduced in length by 6 ft., and the original Avon turbojets have been supplanted by Spey turbofans. The first proto-type powered by Spey engines has been used for aerodynamic investigations, and the second prototype, retaining the original Avon engines, has been used primarily for systems check-out.

HAWKER SIDDELEY NIMROD M.R. MK. 1

Dimensions: Span, 114 ft. 10 in.; length, 127 ft. 0 in.; height, 30 ft. 0 in.; wing area, 2,121 sq. ft.

HAWKER SIDDELEY TRIDENT TWO

Country of Origin: United Kingdom.

Type: Medium-haul Commercial Transport.

Power Plants: Three Rolls-Royce RB.163-25 Spey Mk. 512W turbofans each rated at 11,930 lb.s.t.

Performance: Maximum cruising speed, 606 m.p.h. at 27,000 ft.; long-range cruising speed, 504 m.p.h. at 35,000 ft.; range (at passenger capacity payload), 2,550 mls., (with maximum fuel and 16,600-lb. payload), 3,535 mls.

Weights: Operational empty, 75,800 lb.; maximum loaded, 142,500 lb.

Accommodation: Basic flight crew of three and alternative arrangements for 16 first-class and 67 tourist-class passengers or 115 tourist-class passengers.

Status: In production. First Trident Two flown July 27, 1967, and first deliveries against order for 15 aircraft of this type to B.E.A. scheduled spring 1968.

Notes: The Trident Two differs from the earlier Trident 1C and 1E in having uprated engines, increased weights, flared Küchemann wingtips which cut induced drag and increase overall span by 3 ft., wing and fuselage panels of increased thickness, a strengthened undercarriage, and a 340 Imp. gal. fuel tank in the tail fin. Twenty-three examples of the Trident 1C are operated by B.E.A., and the Trident 1E serves with Iraqi Airways, Pakistan International and Kuwait Airways. In October 1967, five examples of a new 139-passenger version, the Trident 1E-140, were ordered by Channel Airways for delivery from March 1968.

HAWKER SIDDELEY TRIDENT TWO

Dimensions: Span, 98 ft. 0 in.; length, 114 ft. 9 in.; height, 27 ft. 0 in.; wing area, 1,461 sq. ft.

HAWKER SIDDELEY VULCAN B. MK. 2

Country of Origin: United Kingdom.
Type: Long-Range Medium Strategic Bomber.
Power Plants: Four Bristol Siddeley Olympus B.Ol.21 Mk. 301 turbojets each rated at 20,000 lb.s.t.
Performance: (Estimated) Maximum speed, 645 m.p.h. at 40,000–45,000 ft. (Mach 0·98); maximum cruising speed, 620 m.p.h. at 45,000 ft. (Mach 0·94); maximum cruising altitude, 55,000 ft.; tactical radius (for hi-lo-lo-hi sortie profile), 1,700 mls., (at 40,000–55,000 ft.), 2,300 mls.; maximum range, 4,750 mls.
Weights: Loaded, 180,000–200,000 lb.
Armament: One Hawker Siddeley Blue Steel Mk.1 rocket-driven supersonic stand-off missile, or 21 1,000-lb. general-purpose bombs.
Status: Production completed. First B. Mk. 2 flown August 19, 1958, deliveries to R.A.F. Bomber Command commencing July 1960. Production completed 1964.
Notes: Equipping seven R.A.F. Bomber Command Squadrons, the Vulcan B. Mk. 2 was originally conceived for the high-altitude role but its mission capability has now been extended to include low-level penetration, and it is expected to remain in first-line service until the mid-'seventies, although from 1969–1970 its primary role will be tactical. Vulcan B. Mk. 2 was preceded by 45 examples of the B. Mk. 1 with lower-powered turbojets and a smaller wing.

144

HAWKER SIDDELEY VULCAN B. MK. 2

Dimensions: Span, 111 ft. 0 in.; length, 99 ft. 11 in.; height, 27 ft. 2 in.; wing area, 3,964 sq. ft.

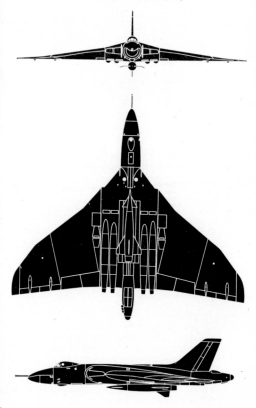

HFB HANSA JET 320

Country of Origin: Federal Germany.

Type: Light Executive Transport.

Power Plants: Two General Electric CJ610-1 turbojets each rated at 2,850 lb.s.t.

Performance: Maximum cruising speed, 495 m.p.h. at 26,250 ft.; time to 26,250 ft., 14 min.; service ceiling (at 17,640 lb.), 37,500 ft.; range (with four passengers and 45 min. reserves), 1,440 mls., (with 11 passengers and 45 min. reserves), 970 mls.

Weights: Basic operational (including two pilots), 12,125 lb.; maximum loaded, 19,400 lb.

Accommodation: Basic flight crew of two and alternative executive layouts for seven and 11 passengers.

Status: In production. First prototype flown April 21, 1964. Initial series of 30 aircraft of which first flown on February 2, 1966. Approximately half of initial batch completed by beginning of 1968.

Notes: Of the initial batch of 30 Hansa Jets, eight have been delivered to the Federal German Defence Ministry's VIP squadron and for use in the military flight test role. The Hansa Jet is unique among current aircraft in having forward-swept wings.

HFB HANSA JET 320

Dimensions: Span, 47 ft. 6⅓ in.; length, 54 ft. 6 in.; height, 16 ft. 2½ in.; wing area, 324·4 sq. ft.

I.A.I. ARAVA

Country of Origin: Israel.

Type: Light Utility Transport.

Power Plants: Two Pratt & Whitney PT6A-27 turbo-props each rated at 620 s.h.p.

Performance: (Estimated) Maximum cruising speed, 224 m.p.h. at 10,000 ft.; economical cruising speed, 186 m.p.h. at 10,000 ft.; initial climb rate, 1,820 ft./min.; service ceiling, 27,900 ft.; range (maximum fuel and 30 min. reserves), 1,120 mls., (maximum payload and 30 min. reserves), 340 mls.

Weights: Operational empty, 7,070 lb.; maximum loaded, 12,500 lb.

Accommodation: Flight crew of one or two and maximum of 20 passengers in four-abreast seating. Alternative layouts for 6–8 passengers, or 12 casualty stretchers and attendants.

Status: Prototype scheduled to fly early 1968.

Notes: Named after a valley in Israel's Negev desert, the Arava is being developed by Israel Aircraft Industries, and is intended to fulfil a variety of roles. A variant with Turboméca Astazou XIV engines is proposed, and for the all-cargo role a full-width rear cargo door hinged to swing sideways will be provided. Construction of a prototype Arava was initiated during 1967.

I.A.I. ARAVA

Dimensions: Span, 68 ft. 7 in.; length, 42 ft. 3 in.; height, 17 ft. 0¾ in.; wing area, 470·2 sq. ft.

ILYUSHIN IL-62 (CLASSIC)

Country of Origin: U.S.S.R.
Type: Long-range Commercial Transport.
Power Plants: Four Kuznetsov NK-8 turbofans each rated at 23,150 lb.s.t.
Performance: Maximum cruising speed, 540 m.p.h. at 32,810 ft.; long-range cruising speed, 520 m.p.h. at 32,810 ft.; range with maximum fuel and 22,046-lb. payload plus one hour's reserves, 5,717 mls., with maximum payload—50,706 lb., 4,163 mls.
Weights: Empty operational, 148,812 lb.; maximum loaded, 340,610 lb.
Accommodation: Flight crew of five and arrangements for 186 passengers in high-density layout, 168 passengers in tourist-class layout, and 115 passengers in first-class layout.
Status: In production. First of two prototypes flown January 1963, production being initiated late in 1965.
Notes: The Il-62 entered service with Aeroflot in 1967, the inaugural Moscow–Montreal Il-62 service being operated on September 15, 1967. The Kuznetsov NK-8 turbofans of the initial production version are scheduled to be supplanted by 25,353 lb.s.t. Soloviev D-30K turbofans during 1968–9. The Il-62 has been subjected to continuous modification during its protracted development.

150

ILYUSHIN IL-62 (CLASSIC)

Dimensions: Span, 142 ft. 0¾ in.; length, 174 ft. 2½ in.;
height, 40 ft. 8 in.; wing area, 3,037·57 sq. ft.

KAWASAKI P-2J

Country of Origin: Japan.

Type: Long-Range Maritime Patrol Aircraft.

Power Plants: Two General Electric T64-IHI-10 turboprops each rated at 2,850 e.s.h.p., and two Ishikawajima-Harima J3-IHI-7C turbojets each rated at 3,086 lb.s.t.

Performance: Approximate maximum speed (all engines), 350 m.p.h. at 20,000 ft., (turboprops only), 300 m.p.h.; long-range cruising speed, 230 m.p.h.; service ceiling, 40,000 ft.; take-off distance (to clear 50 ft.), 2,200 ft.; landing distance (from 50 ft.), 2,160 ft.

Weights: Empty, 44,974 lb.; normal loaded, 74,957 lb.

Armament: Two 2,165-lb. torpedoes, two 2,000-lb. mines, or eight 1,000-lb. mines or bombs.

Accommodation: Total crew of twelve.

Status: Under development. Prototype flown July 21, 1966. Current plans call for manufacture of 68 with first production model flying spring 1968.

Notes: Evolved from the Lockheed SP-2H Neptune, 48 examples of which have been manufactured under licence in Japan by Kawasaki, the GK-210, or P-2J, differs from its predecessor in having the piston engines replaced by turboprops and auxiliary turbojets of indigenous design. A 45-in. section has been added to the forward fuselage, X-band APS-80A search radar replaces the APS-20, twin-wheel main undercarriage members have been introduced.

152

KAWASAKI P-2J

Dimensions: Span, 101 ft. 4¾ in.; length, 96 ft. 1½ in.; height, 29 ft. 2½ in.; wing area, 1,000 sq. ft.

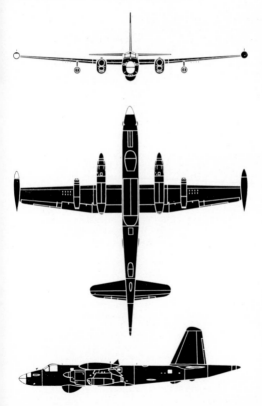

LING-TEMCO-VOUGHT A-7A CORSAIR II

Country of Origin: U.S.A.

Type: Single-seat Light Shipboard Attack Bomber.

Power Plant: One Pratt & Whitney TF30-P-6 turbofan rated at 11,350 lb.s.t.

Performance: Maximum speed (without external stores), 690 m.p.h. at sea level, (with 3,600-lb. external bomb and fuel load), 585 m.p.h.; long-range cruising speed (without external stores), 542 m.p.h. at 40,000 ft.; tactical radius (with 3,600 lb. external ordnance, no external fuel and including 265 mls. at sea level), 810 mls.; ferry range (maximum external fuel), 3,050 mls.

Weights: Empty, 14,857 lb.; loaded (clean), 26,400 lb.; maximum catapult weight, 32,500 lb.; maximum overload, 35,650 lb.

Armament: Two 20-mm. cannon with 250 r.p.g. and provision for up to 15,000 lb. ordnance on eight stations.

Status: (A-7A) Production completed with last of 199 delivered December 1967. (A-7B) in production with deliveries against orders for 196 initiated January 1968. Current U.S. Navy planned procurement of 1,138 Corsair IIs of all versions.

Notes: A-7B differs from -7A in having 12,000 lb.s.t. TF30-P-8 engine. A-7E (of which 151 ordered under Fiscal 1967–8 contracts) will have updated avionics and M-61 rotary cannon. A-7F is proposed version with 15,000 lb.s.t. TF30-P-18P engine, and A-7D is U.S.A.F. model with 14,250 lb.s.t. Allison TF41-A-1 (Spey 201) and M-61 cannon for 1969 delivery.

LING-TEMCO-VOUGHT A-7A CORSAIR II

Dimensions: Span, 38 ft. 8¾ in.; length, 46 ft. 1½ in.; height, 16 ft. 2 in.; wing area, 375 sq. ft.

LOCKHEED C-5A GALAXY

Country of Origin: U.S.A.

Type: Long-range Military Strategic Transport.

Power Plants: Four General Electric TF39-GE-1 turbofans each rated at 41,000 lb.s.t.

Performance: (Estimated) Maximum cruising speed, 540 m.p.h.; economical cruising speed, 506 m.p.h.; initial climb rate (at 712,000 lb.), 2,100 ft./min.; range (with 220,000-lb. payload), 3,510 mls., (with 112,600-lb. payload), 6,330 mls.; ferry range, 8,290 mls.

Weights: Operational empty, 323,904 lb.; maximum loaded, 764,500 lb.

Accommodation: Flight crew of six plus relief crew of six, courier seating for eight plus 75 troops in upper compartment above cargo hold. Maximum payload of 265,000 lb.

Status: In production. First C-5A scheduled to fly June 1968 with first delivery to the U.S.A.F. Military Airlift Command following in June 1969. Total of 58 aircraft ordered by November 1, 1967, with options on a further 143.

Notes: Current planning calls for six C-5A squadrons of 16 aircraft, and several variants of the basic design have been proposed, including airborne command and control post, and airborne strategic missile launcher.

156

LOCKHEED C-5A GALAXY

Dimensions: Span, 222 ft. 7¼ in.; length, 245 ft. 10¾ in.;
height, 65 ft. 1¼ in.; wing area, 6,200 sq. ft.

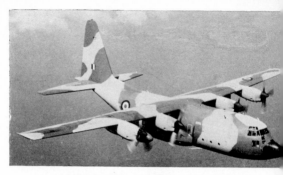

LOCKHEED C-130K HERCULES

Country of Origin: U.S.A.

Type: Military Strategic Transport.

Power Plants: Four Allison T56-A-15 turboprops each rated at 4,910 e.s.h.p.

Performance: Maximum cruising speed, 385 m.p.h.; normal cruising speed, 340 m.p.h.; initial climb rate (at 155,000 lb.), 1,880 ft./min.; range (maximum payload—45,901 lb.), 2,430 mls., (maximum fuel and 20,259-lb. payload), 4,780 mls.

Weight: Maximum loaded, 155,000 lb.

Accommodation: Normal crew of five plus 92 troops, 62 paratroops, or 74 casualty stretchers plus two medical attendants.

Status: In production. First C-130K flew October 19, 1966, initial contracts calling for 66 aircraft of this type, with completion of deliveries by early 1968. Approximately 960 C-130s of all types delivered by the beginning of 1968, when 1,036 had been ordered with production running at five per month.

Notes: C-130K is version for R.A.F. for which some sub-assembles have been manufactured by Scottish Aviation in the U.K. The C-130K is essentially similar to the C-130H for the R.N.Z.A.F., and, apart from the power plants, to the C-130E which is the principal U.S.A.F. version.

158

LOCKHEED C-130K HERCULES

Dimensions: Span, 132 ft. 7¼ in.; length, 99 ft. 6 in.; height, 38 ft. 3½ in.; wing area, 1,745 sq. ft.

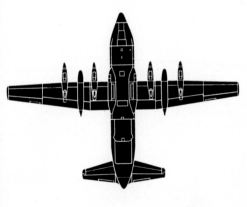

LOCKHEED C-141A STARLIFTER

Country of Origin: U.S.A.
Type: Military Strategic Transport.
Power Plants: Four Pratt & Whitney TF33-P-7 turbofans each rated at 21,000 lb.s.t.
Performance: Maximum speed, 570 m.p.h.; maximum cruising speed, 562 m.p.h.; long-range cruising speed, 506 m.p.h.; initial climb rate, 3,200 ft./min.; service ceiling (at 250,000 lb.), 40,000 ft.; range (with 70,847-lb. payload), 3,973 mls., (with maximum fuel and 30,877-lb. payload), 6,045 mls.; ferry, 6,822 mls.
Weights: Empty equipped, 133,773 lb.; max. loaded, 316,100 lb.
Accommodation: Normal flight crew of four, and a maximum of 154 troops, 123 paratroops, or 80 casualty stretchers and eight medical attendants.   Up to 5,283 cu. ft. of freight may be loaded on 10 pallets.
Status: In production.   First test and evaluation aircraft flown December 17, 1963, and first delivery to U.S.A.F. Military Airlift Command on October 20, 1964.   Total orders placed call for 248 aircraft, the last of which was scheduled to be delivered in February 1968.
Notes: The StarLifter equips 14 Military Airlift Command squadrons, the last of which, the 30th Military Airlift Squadron, began re-equipping in August 1967.   At the time of closing for press, it was anticipated that three StarLifters would be ordered for the Canadian Defence Forces.   A proposed commercial counterpart of the C-141A is the Model 300-101.

LOCKHEED C-141A STARLIFTER

Dimensions: Span, 160 ft. 1 in.; length, 145 ft. 0 in.;
height, 39 ft. 4 in.; wing area, 3,228 sq. ft.

LOCKHEED F-104S STARFIGHTER

Country of Origin: U.S.A.

Type: Single-seat Interceptor and Strike Fighter.

Power Plant: One General Electric J79-GE-19 turbojet rated at 11,870 lb.s.t. and 17,900 lb.s.t. with afterburning.

Performance: Maximum speed, 1,450 m.p.h. at 40,000 ft. (Mach 2·2), 915 m.p.h. at 1,000 ft. (Mach 1·2); cruising speed, 610 m.p.h. at 36,000 ft. (Mach 0·92); initial climb rate, 50,000+ ft./min.; combat ceiling, 57,000 ft.; tactical radius (with two 162 Imp. gal./200 U.S. gal. and two 100 Imp. gal./120 U.S. gal. drop tanks), 740–775 mls.; ferry range, 2,200 mls.

Weights: (Estimated) Empty, 14,500 lb.; loaded (clean), 20,000 lb.; max. loaded, 29,500 lb.

Armament: One 20-mm. M-61 Vulcan rotary cannon and two AIM-7 Sparrow III semi-active radar homing and two AIM-9 Sidewinder infra-red homing AAMs.

Status: In production. First of two F-104S prototypes commenced flight test programme in December 1966. Production of 165 being undertaken in Italy with first deliveries scheduled for mid-1968 and current order being completed in 1971.

Notes: The F-104S is a derivative of the F-104G (see 1966 edition) intended primarily for the all-weather intercept role. Two prototypes have been modified by the parent company from Italian-manufactured F-104G airframes, and licence manufacture is being undertaken for the Italian Air Force by Fiat. The F-104S offers a 37% improvement in transonic acceleration, improved manœuvrability and a four per cent increase in combat ceiling.

162

LOCKHEED F-104S STARFIGHTER

Dimensions: Span, 21 ft. 11 in.; length, 54 ft. 9 in.;
height, 13 ft. 6 in.; wing area, 196·1 sq. ft.

LOCKHEED P-3B ORION

Country of Origin: U.S.A.

Type: Long-range Maritime Patrol Aircraft.

Power Plants: Four Allison T56-A-14 turboprops each rated at 4,910 e.s.h.p. (4,591 s.h.p.).

Performance: (At 105,000 lb.) Maximum speed, 476 m.p.h. at 15,000 ft.; normal cruising speed, 397 m.p.h. at 25,000 ft.; initial climb rate, 3,270 ft./min.; loiter endurance (four engines) at 1,500 ft., 12·9 hr., (two engines), 17 hr.; maximum mission radius (3 hr. on station at 1,500 ft.), 2,533 mls.

Weights: Empty, 60,000 lb.; max. loaded, 127,200 lb.

Accommodation: Normal crew of 12 comprising pilot, co-pilot, flight engineer, radio operator, navigator, sonobuoy operator, radar/MAD operator, Julie/ECM operator, tactical co-ordinator, ordnanceman, and two relief members, and for emergency troop carrier role up to 50 combat troops and 4,000 lb. of equipment may be accommodated by removal of sonobuoy stowage racks and installation of combat seats.

Armament: Weapons bay can accommodate two Mk. 101 nuclear depth bombs and four Mk. 43, 44 or 46 torpedoes, or eight Mk. 54 bombs. All 10 external pylons can carry torpedoes, mines or rockets, maximum external stores load being 13,713 lb.

Status: In production. YP-3A prototype flown on November 25, 1959, and first pre-production P-3A flown April 15, 1961. More than 250 delivered by end of 1967.

Notes: P-3B ordered by R.N.Z.A.F. (5) and R.A.A.F. (10). The P-3C will feature advanced avionics, maximum and overload weights of 133,500 lb. and 142,000 lb. and will be delivered from January 1969.

LOCKHEED P-3B ORION

Dimensions: Span, 99 ft. 8 in.; length, 116 ft. 10 in.; height, 33 ft. 8½ in.; wing area, 1,300 sq. ft.

McDONNELL F-4E PHANTOM II

Country of Origin: U.S.A.

Type: Two-seat Tactical Strike Fighter.

Power Plants: Two General Electric J79-GE-17 turbo-jets each rated at 11,870 lb.s.t. and 17,900 lb.s.t. with afterburning.

Performance: Maximum speed (without external stores), 1,580 m.p.h. at 40,000 ft. (Mach 2·4), 910 m.p.h. at sea level (Mach 1·2); initial climb rate, 30,000 ft./min.; low-level tactical radius (eight 750 lb. bombs and two 308 Imp. gal. drop tanks), 400 mls. at 420 m.p.h.; ferry range, 2,300 mls. at 575 m.p.h. at 40,000 ft.

Weights: Approx. empty, 30,000 lb.; max. loaded, 59,000 lb.

Armament: One 20-mm. General Electric M-61A1 rotary cannon and up to 16,000 lb. of external stores, typical loads including 15 1,000-lb. Mk. 83, 18 750-lb. M-117, or 24 500-lb. Mk. 82 bombs, four AGM-12 Bullpup ASMs, or 15 LAU-3A or 13 LAU-10A rocket launchers.

Status: In production. First F-4E flown on June 30, 1967, and first to U.S.A.F. on October 3, 1967.

Notes: The F-4E is the production successor to the F-4D (see 1967 edition) from which it differs in having an extended nose housing an improved and miniaturised APQ-120 fire control radar system and recessed pod with a multiple-barrel M-61A1 cannon, uprated engines and an additional fuel cell.

166

McDONNELL F-4E PHANTOM II

Dimensions: Span, 38 ft. 4¾ in.; length, 62 ft. 10 in.; height, 16 ft. 3 in.; wing area, 530 sq. ft.

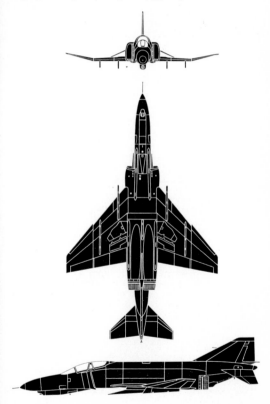

McDONNELL F-4M PHANTOM II

Country of Origin: U.S.A.

Type: Two-seat Strike and Reconnaissance Fighter.

Power Plants: Two Rolls-Royce RB.168–25R Spey R.Sp. 5R Mk. 201 turbofans each rated at 12,500 lb.s.t. and 20,100 lb.s.t. with afterburning.

Performance: Maximum speed (with four AIM-7E Sparrow III AAMs), 1,386 m.p.h. at 40,000 ft. (Mach 2·1), 910 m.p.h. at sea level (Mach 1·2); service ceiling, 60,000 ft.; low-level tactical radius (with six 1,000-lb. bombs or equivalent external load), 500 mls.; ferry range, 2,500 mls.

Weights: Approx. empty, 30,000 lb.; maximum loaded, 56,000 lb.

Armament: (Strike) Combinations of missiles, such as the AS.37 and AJ.168 Martel, AGM-12 Bullpup, etc., and bombs. (Intercept) Four or six AIM-7E Sparrow III semi-active radar-homing AAMs.

Status: In production. The first of two YF-4M prototypes flown on February 17, 1967. Current orders call for 98 F-4Ms of which first to be delivered to R.A.F. early 1968.

Notes: Anglicised shore-based equivalent of U.S. Navy's F-4J and essentially similar to F-4K (see 1967 edition) shipboard strike fighter for Royal Navy. Two YF-4Ks and 48 F-4Ks ordered with initial deliveries for early 1968. The F-4M has either dual controls or reconnaissance controls in rear cockpit, the latter being used with a British pod for sensors, thus providing reconnaissance capability while retaining air superiority and attack capability.

168

McDONNELL F-4M PHANTOM II

Dimensions: Span, 38 ft. 4 in.; length, 57 ft. 11 in.; height, 16 ft. 3⅓ in.; wing area, 530 sq. ft.

MIKOYAN MIG-21PF (FISHBED-D)

Country of Origin: U.S.S.R.

Type: Single-seat All-weather Interceptor Fighter.

Power Plant: One TDR R.37F turbojet rated at approximately 10,000 lb.s.t and 13,200 lb.s.t. with afterburning.

Performance: Maximum speed (without external stores), 1,450 m.p.h. at 36,000–40,000 ft. (Mach 2·2), (with two Atoll AAMs or UV-16-57 rocket pods), 1,320 m.p.h. (Mach 2·0); subsonic cruise tactical radius (without external fuel), 400 mls.; time to 40,000 ft., 4·5 min.

Weights: (Estimated) loaded (with one 132 Imp. gal. centreline drop tank and two Atoll missiles), 17,700 lb.; maximum loaded, 19,500 lb.

Armament: Two Atoll AAMs or two UV-16-57 pods each housing 16 55-mm. rockets.

Status: In production. Licence manufacture undertaken in Czechoslovakia and India (latter producing MiG-21FL).

Notes: In its latest form, the MiG-21PF embodies a number of modifications (illustrated by the photograph above and the drawing on the opposite page), including vertical tail surfaces of increased chord, a repositioned braking chute housing, and a new cockpit canopy with separate quarter lights and hood. The export version of the MiG-21PF, the MiG-21FL, differs from the standard model only in avionic equipment, and the MiG-21F (Fishbed-C) is the standard day interceptor model.

MIKOYAN MIG-21PF (FISHBED-D)

Estimated Dimensions: Span, 25 ft. 0 in.; length, 49 ft.
0 in.; height, 15 ft. 0 in.; wing area, 250 sq. ft.

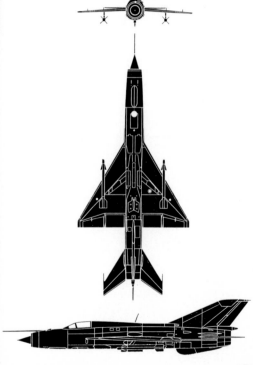

MIG-21UTI (MONGOL)

Country of Origin: U.S.S.R.

Type: Tandem Two-seat Advanced and Combat Proficiency Trainer.

Power Plant: One axial-flow turbojet rated at approximately 9,500 lb.s.t. and 12,500 lb.s.t. with afterburning.

Performance: Approximate maximum speed (clean), 1,385 m.p.h. above 36,000 ft. (Mach 2·1), (with two AAMs and one 132 Imp. gal. drop tank), 990 m.p.h. (Mach 1·5); approx. initial climb rate, 35,000 ft./min.; service ceiling, 60,000+ ft.; tactical radius (clean), 250–300 mls.

Weights: Approximate loaded (clean), 17,500 lb.; maximum loaded, 19,000 lb.

Armament: Two Atoll infra-red homing AAMs.

Status: In production. Prototype believed flown 1963.

Notes: Successor to the MiG-15UTI (Midget), the MiG-21UTI differs from the standard MiG-21F single-seat day interceptor (see 1967 edition) primarily in having a second cockpit inserted aft at some expense to fuel capacity. Unlike the interceptor's windscreen which is attached to the canopy and hinged at the forward edge for access, that of the MiG-21UTI is fixed, separate starboard-hinging glazed sections enclosing the tandem cockpits. The cannon armament of the day fighter version is not normally retained by the trainer, but provision is made for an infra-red homing missile beneath each wing. The MiG-21UTI is now standard advanced training equipment in the Soviet Air Forces, pupils progressing to this type from the L-29 (Maya) basic trainer.

172

MIG-21UTI (MONGOL)

Estimated Dimensions: Span, 25 ft. 0 in.; length, 47 ft.
0 in.; height, 14 ft. 6 in.; wing area, 250 sq. ft.

MIKOYAN FLOGGER

Country of Origin: U.S.S.R.

Type: Single-seat Tactical Strike and Reconnaissance Fighter.

Power Plant: One turbojet rated at 28,000–30,000 lb. s.t. with afterburning.

Performance: (Estimated) Maximum speed, 1,650 m.p.h. at 40,000 ft. (Mach 2·5), 910 m.p.h. at sea level (Mach 1·2).

Weights: Approximate loaded, 40,000–45,000 lb.

Status: Believed experimental. Single prototype demonstrated at Domodedovo July 1967. Current status uncertain. Possible service introduction 1969–1970.

Notes: Appreciably smaller and lighter than the General Dynamics F-111 and approximating more closely to the Dassault Mirage G, the Mikoyan-designed variable-geometry fighter was believed to have attained a relatively early development stage at the time of closing for press. The wing design follows U.S. first generation practice closely in that the hinge points are set well out from the fuselage and large fixed wing-root gloves are provided. The wing reportedly translates from the full-forward low-speed position to the full-aft high-speed position in some four seconds. The rectangular air intakes are noteworthy, and the vertical tail surfaces are augmented at high speeds by a large ventral fin which appears to fold sideways for take-off and landing.

174

MIKOYAN FLOGGER

Estimated Dimensions: Span (minimum sweep), 48 ft.
0 in., (maximum sweep), 24 ft. 0 in.; length (including
probe), 60 ft. 0 in.; height, 15 ft. 0 in.

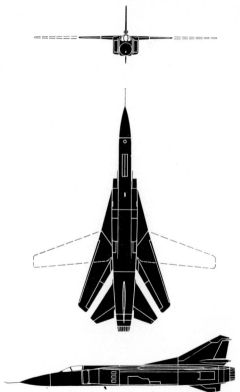

MIKOYAN MIG-23 (FOXBAT)

Country of Origin: U.S.S.R.

Type: Single-seat Interceptor and Strike Fighter.

Power Plants: Two turbojets each rated at approx. 22,000 lb.s.t. and 33,000 lb.s.t. with afterburning.

Performance: (Estimated) Maximum speed (short-period dash), 2,110 m.p.h. at 40,000–50,000 ft. (Mach 3·2), 910 m.p.h. at sea level (Mach 1·2).

Weights: Approximate loaded, 100,000 lb.

Status: In production. Believed flown in prototype form 1963–64 with first service deliveries 1966.

Notes: The Foxbat, designated MiG-23 in service form, has established a number of internationally-recognised records as the Ye-266, the first of these being announced in April 1965 and being a 1,000-km. closed-circuit record of 1,441·5 m.p.h. (Mach 2·2) carrying a 4,409-lb. payload, the flight being performed between 69,000 and 72,200 ft. In October 1967, the Ye-266 attained 98,458 ft. with a 4,409-lb. payload and covered a 500-km. closed circuit at an average speed of 1,820·6 m.p.h. (Mach 2·76), and on November 4, 1967 averaged 1,807 m.p.h. over a 1,000-km. circuit.

MIKOYAN MIG-23 (FOXBAT)

Estimated Dimensions: Span, 47 ft. 0 in.; length, 85 ft. 0 ins.; height, 20 ft. 0 in.; wing area, 830 sq. ft.

MIKOYAN FAITHLESS

Country of Origin: U.S.S.R.
Type: Single-seat S.T.O.L. Fighter-Bomber.
Power Plants: One turbojet of 25,000–30,000 lb.s.t. with afterburning and two vertically-disposed lift engines.
Performance: Presumed to be capable of speeds of the order of Mach 2·2–2·5.
Weights: Believed to be in the 40,000–45,000 lb. loaded weight category.
Status: Believed experimental. Prototypes probably tested during 1966–7, but this type is not believed to have attained production status.
Notes: This short take-off and landing single-seat fighter bomber made its public début at Domodedovo on July 9, 1967, when a single prototype was demonstrated. In addition to the single large cruise engine, two vertical lift engines are mounted in the fuselage aft of the cockpit to reduce take-off and landing runs, but there is some evidence to suggest that development was initiated as a conventional type, the lift engines being added as a second phase.

178

MIKOYAN FAITHLESS

Estimated Dimensions: Span, 30 ft. 0 in.; length (including nose probe), 62 ft. 0 in.; height, 15 ft. 0 in.

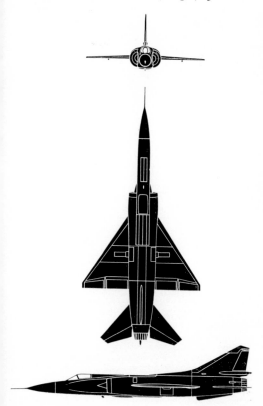

MITSUBISHI MU-2B

Country of Origin: Japan.
Type: Light Executive and Utility Transport.
Power Plants: Two Garrett AiResearch TPE-331-25A turboprops each rated at 575 s.h.p.
Performance: Maximum cruising speed, 310 m.p.h. at 10,000 ft.; economical cruising speed, 273 m.p.h. at 20,000 ft.; initial climb rate, 2,220 ft./min.; service ceiling, 26,000 ft.; maximum range (with 30 min. reserves), 1,200 mls. at 20,000 ft.
Weights: Empty, 5,340 lb.; maximum loaded, 8,930 lb.
Accommodation: Standard version provides pressurised cabin for pilot and six passengers. Alternative arrangement provides accommodation for eight passengers.
Status: In production. First prototype (MU-2A) flown September 14, 1963, and first MU-2B flown on March 11, 1965. Production was scheduled to attain eight per month by the end of 1967.
Notes: Illustrated above is the MU-2C tactical reconnaissance and liaison model for the Ground Self-Defence Force, equipped with two cameras and two 12·7-mm. machine guns. Of 20 MU-2Cs to be delivered five will have side-looking radar and five will have infra-red detection equipment. A variant, the MU-2D flown during 1966, differs from the MU-2B in having integral-type fuel tanks. The Air Self-Defence Force has a requirement for 20 rescue and liaison models designated MU-2E.
180

MITSUBISHI MU-2B

Dimensions: Span, 39 ft. 2 in.; length, 33 ft. 3 in.; height, 12 ft. 11 in.; wing area, 178 sq. ft.

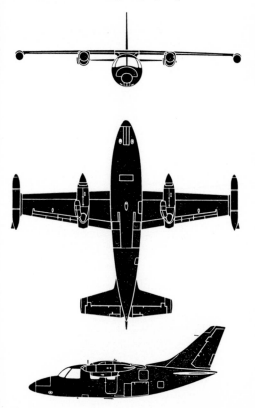

NAMC YS-11

Country of Origin: Japan.

Type: Short- and Medium-range Commercial Transport.

Power Plants: Two Rolls-Royce Dart 542-10 turboprops rated at 2,660 e.h.p. (dry) and 3,060 e.h.p. (wet).

Performance: (Figures in parentheses relate to YS-11A) Maximum cruising speed, 297 (294) m.p.h. at 15,000 ft.; economical cruising speed, 290 (287) m.p.h. at 20,000 ft.; long-range cruising speed, 245 m.p.h. at 20,000 ft.; initial climb rate, 1,320 ft./min.; service ceiling, 27,500 ft.; range (with maximum fuel and 5,840-lb. payload and reserves), 1,440 (1,405) mls., (with maximum payload), 340 (220) mls.

Weights: Empty, 32,165 (32,300) lb.; maximum loaded, 51,800 (54,010) lb.

Accommodation: Flight crew of two plus cabin crew, and 52–60 passengers in pairs on each side of aisle.

Status: In production. First prototype flown on August 30, 1962, followed by second prototype on December 28, 1962. First deliveries effected March 1965, and 53 were scheduled to have been completed by the beginning of 1968, including four YS-11As. First YS-11A was scheduled to be completed late 1967.

Notes: Variants of the YS-11 include the YS-11P personnel carrier for the J.A.S.D.F., the YS-11M convertible personnel freight and passenger transport for the J.M.S.D.F., and the YS-11A which is planned in three versions: the all-passenger Srs. 200, the mixed freight-and-cargo Srs. 300, and the all-cargo Srs. 400.

182

NAMC YS-11

Dimensions: Span, 104 ft. 11¾ in.; length, 86 ft. 3½ in.;
height, 29 ft. 5¾ in.; wing area, 1,020·4 sq. ft.

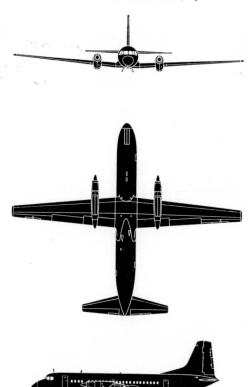

NEIVA L-42 REGENTE

Country of Origin: Brazil.

Type: Light Air Observation Post and Army Co-operation Monoplane.

Power Plant: One Lycoming O-360-A1D four-cylinder horizontally-opposed engine rated at 180 h.p.

Performance: Maximum speed, 155 m.p.h. at 3,280 ft.; cruising speed at 75% power, 135 m.p.h. at 6,500 ft.; economical cruising speed at 68% power, 123 m.p.h.; initial climb rate, 880 ft./min.; service ceiling, 19,000 ft.; range at economical cruise, 740 mls.

Weights: Empty equipped, 1,411 lb.; maximum loaded, 2,293 lb.

Accommodation: Standard accommodation for pilot and observer but provision for single casualty stretcher.

Status: Prototype (YL-42) trials initiated early 1967 with production deliveries against initial order for 20 L-42s scheduled for early 1968.

Notes: Developed from C-42 Regente four-seat utility monoplane, 60 examples of which have been delivered to the Brazilian Air Force, the L-42 has been evolved to meet a requirement for a replacement for the Cessna O-1 Bird Dog and Neiva L-6 in Brazilian service. The L-42 differs from the C-42 in having a redesigned cockpit canopy, cut-down rear fuselage, and wheels of larger diameter for improved rough-field operation.

NEIVA L-42 REGENTE

Dimensions: Span, 29 ft. $11\frac{1}{2}$ in.; length, 23 ft. $1\frac{1}{4}$ in.; height, 9 ft. $7\frac{1}{3}$ in.; wing area, 144·8 sq. ft.

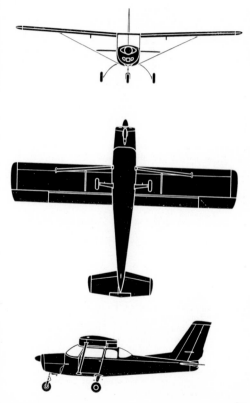

NORD 262

Country of Origin: France.

Type: Light Commercial Transport.

Power Plants: Two Turboméca Bastan VIC turbo-props each rated at 1,065 e.s.h.p.

Performance: Maximum speed, 239 m.p.h. at 14,990 ft.; economical cruising speed (70% power), 224 m.p.h. at 16,400 ft.; initial climb rate, 1,160 ft./min.; service ceiling, 24,000 ft.; range (maximum fuel and 4,426-lb. payload), 690 mls., (with maximum payload —6,400 lb.), 200 mls.

Weights: Empty operational, 15,123 lb.; maximum loaded, 22,707 lb.

Accommodation: Crew of two and seating for 26 passengers in standard version. Alternative arrangements available for 29 passengers. Movable bulkhead caters for variable cargo-passenger configuration.

Status: In production. Prototype flown December 24, 1962, and first production model flown May 7, 1963. First production aircraft to definitive standards flown on June 10, 1964. Production of 70 authorised, and production rate was being increased from one to two per month by mid-1968.

Notes: Intended as a potential DC-3 replacement, the pressurised Nord 262 is currently operated by Air Inter, Lake Central, and Japan Domestic Airlines, and other purchasers include Alisarda, Air Ceylon and Air Madagascar, and France's *Aéronavale* has ordered 15 and taken an option on a further 16 for light transport and crew training tasks.

186

NORD 262

Dimensions: Span, 71 ft. $10\frac{1}{4}$ in.; length, 63 ft. 3 in.;
height, 20 ft. 4 in.; wing area, 592 sq. ft.

NORD 500

Country of Origin: France.
Type: Single-seat Tilt-duct VTOL Research Aircraft.
Power Plants: Two Allison T63-A-5 shaft turbines each
rated at 317 s.h.p.
Performance: (Estimated) Maximum speed, 217 m.p.h.
at sea level; cruising speed, 175 m.p.h.
Weights: Maximum loaded, 2,760 lb.
Status: Prototype development. First prototype began
static tests in April 1967, and second prototype was
scheduled to commence the hovering test programme
at the beginning of 1968.
Notes: The Nord 500 tilting-duct research aircraft
is of generally similar concept to the Bell X-22A
(see 1966 edition). The short-span fixed surfaces are
carried by a raised boom which also houses the
side-by-side T63-A-5 shaft turbines driving the
five-bladed ducted airscrews via interconnected shafts.
For vertical take-off and landing the ducts are tilted
to horizontal position. Conventional cockpit controls
are provided, control in yaw and pitch being achieved
by differential and collective duct tilting respectively,
and thrust modulation being employed for roll
control.

NORD 500

Dimensions: Span, 20 ft. 1½ in.; length, 21 ft. 7 in.; height, 10 ft. 1½ in.

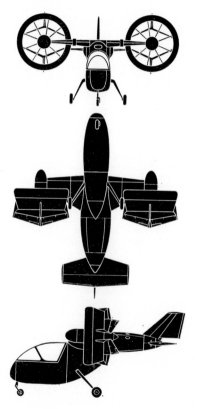

NORTH AMERICAN OV-10A BRONCO

Country of Origin: U.S.A.
Type: Two-seat Forward Air Control and Lighter Counter Insurgency Aircraft.
Power Plants: Two Garrett AiResearch T76-G-10/12 turboprops each rated at 715 s.h.p.
Performance: Maximum speed, 279 m.p.h. at sea level, 259 m.p.h. at 20,000 ft.; average cruising speed, 194 m.p.h.; initial climb rate, 2,320 ft./min.; tactical radius (close support strike mission at 12,500 lb. with one hour loiter in target area), 110 mls. with 146 Imp. gal., 210 mls. with 210 Imp. gal., 390 mls. with 335 Imp. gal.; ferry range, 1,310 mls.
Weights: Empty, 7,076 lb.; normal loaded, 11,340 lb.; maximum, 12,500 lb.
Armament: Four 7·62-mm. M-60C machine guns with 500 r.p.g. One 1,200-lb. and four 600-lb. capacity external stations, and (USMC version) two wing pylons for AIM-9D Sidewinder missiles.
Status: First of seven prototypes flown July 16, 1965, and first production aircraft flown August 6, 1967. Current contracts call for 109 aircraft for the U.S.A.F. and 76 for U.S.M.C., and long-lead procurement has been made for a further 38 aircraft for the U.S.M.C.
Notes: The Bronco is scheduled to enter service with both the U.S.A.F. and U.S.M.C. during 1968.

NORTH AMERICAN OV-10A BRONCO

Dimensions: Span, 40 ft. 0 in.; length (including pitot head), 41 ft. 7 in.; height, 15 ft. 1 in.; wing area, 291 sq. ft.

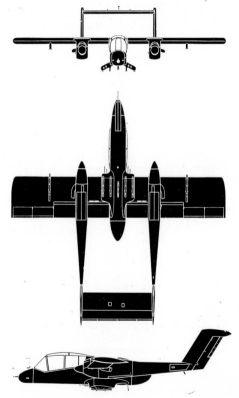

NORTH AMERICAN RA-5C VIGILANTE

Country of Origin: U.S.A.
Type: Tandem Two-seat Shipboard Strategic Reconnaissance and Attack Bomber.
Power Plants: Two General Electric J79-GE-8 turbojets each rated at 10,900 lb.s.t. and 17,000 lb. with afterburning.
Performance: Maximum speed, 1,385 m.p.h. at 40,000 ft. (Mach 2·1); maximum stabilised speed (without external stores), 1,254 m.p.h. (Mach 1·9); maximum low-level cruising speed, 633 m.p.h. (Mach 0·83); long-range cruising speed, 560 m.p.h. at 40,000 ft. (Mach 0·85); operational ceiling, 64,000 ft.; maximum range, 2,995 mls.
Weights: Loaded, 61,730 lb.; max. overload, 74,000 lb.
Armament: The RA-5C normally fulfils the reconnaissance role but possesses secondary attack capability, each of four external pylons being capable of lifting a 2,500-lb. load of offensive stores.
Status: Production reinstated in 1967. Prototype RA-5C flown June 30, 1962. Remaining A-5A Vigilantes subsequently being brought up to RA-5C standards.
Notes: Serving with six U.S. Navy Reconnaissance Attack Squadrons, the RA-5C carries an extremely sophisticated reconnaissance system, including vertical, oblique, and split-image cameras, and SLAR (Side-Looking Airborne Radar) in removable modules. Production originally terminated in 1963, all A-5As subsequently being converted as RA-5Cs.

NORTH AMERICAN RA-5C VIGILANTE

Dimensions: Span, 53 ft. 0 in.; length, 75 ft. 10 in.;
height, 19 ft. 4¾ in.; wing area, 700 sq. ft.

NORTH AMERICAN SABRELINER SRS. 60

Country of Origin: U.S.A.

Type: Light Executive Transport.

Power Plants: Two Pratt & Whitney JT12A-8 turbo-jets each rated at 3,300 lb.s.t.

Performance: Maximum speed, 563 m.p.h. (Mach 0·85) at 35,000 ft.; maximum cruising speed, 530 m.p.h. (Mach 0·8) at 35,000 ft.; economical cruising speed, 470 m.p.h.; time to 35,000 ft., 17 min.; maximum range with capacity payload, 1,950 mls.

Weights: Basic, 10,486 lb.; max. loaded, 19,615 lb.

Accommodation: Flight crew of two and various internal arrangements for maximum of 10 passengers.

Status: In production. Series 60 first announced January 1967, FAA certification acquired May 1967.

Notes: The Sabreliner was originally developed to meet a U.S.A.F. requirement for a combat readiness trainer and utility aircraft, 191 subsequently being produced under the designation T-39. Current commercial production models are the Srs. 40 and Srs. 60, the former having been announced in June 1966, and both having the JT12A-8A in place of the 3,000 lb.s.t. JT12A-6A of earlier commercial versions. The Sabreliner Srs. 40 is similar to the Srs. 60 apart from overall fuselage length (43 ft. 9½ in.) and passenger capacity (restricted to maximum of seven), maximum take-off weight being 18,650 lb. The 38-in. addition to the fuselage of the Srs. 60 increases interior space by 25 per cent.

194

NORTH AMERICAN SABRELINER SRS. 60

Dimensions: Span, 44 ft. 4¾ in.; length, 48 ft. 4 in.; height, 16 ft. 0 in.; wing area, 342·1 sq. ft.

NORTHROP F-5A

Country of Origin: U.S.A.
Type: Single-seat Strike and Reconnaissance Fighter.
Power Plants: Two General Electric J85-GE-13 turbojets each rated at 2,720 lb.s.t. and 4,080 lb.s.t. with afterburning.
Performance: Maximum speed (without external ordnance), 924 m.p.h. at 36,860 ft. (Mach 1·4), (with wingtip Sidewinder AAMs), 870 m.p.h. (Mach 1·32); long-range cruising speed (maximum fuel configuration), 554 m.p.h. at 36,000–40,000 ft. (Mach 0·84); initial climb rate (without external stores), 29,800 ft./min.; tactical radius (supersonic intercept mission with Mach 1·24 cruise to intercept point, 5 min. max. power and Mach 0·84 return), 167 mls., (attack mission with 458 Imp. gal./550 U.S. gal. auxiliary fuel and 1,500 lb. ordnance), 635 mls.; ferry range, 1,865 mls.
Weights: Empty, 7,860 lb.; max. loaded, 20,040 lb.
Armament: Two 20-mm. M-39 cannon with 280 r.p.g. and maximum external ordnance load of 6,200 lb.
Status: In production. First of three prototypes flown July 30, 1959. First MAP production F-5A flown May 19, 1964. Some 500 F-5s delivered by beginning of 1967 when plans called for manufacture of 750–800 MAP F-5s through 1968–69, the ratio of two-seat F-5Bs to single-seat F-5As being approximately 1 : 9. Licence manufacture in Canada by Canadair (for Canadian Defence Force's Mobile Command) of 115 as single-seat CF-5A and two-seat CF-5D with deliveries for early 1968. Canadair also participating in production of 105 F-5s for The Netherlands.

NORTHROP F-5A

Dimensions: Span, 25 ft. 3 in.; length, 47 ft. 2⅓ in.; height, 13 ft. 2 in.; wing area, 173·82 sq. ft.

PILATUS PC-8 TWIN-PORTER

Country of Origin: Switzerland.

Type: Light STOL Utility Transport.

Power Plants: Two Lycoming IO-540-G1B5 six-cylinder horizontally-opposed engines each rated at 290 h.p.

Performance: (Estimated) Maximum speed, 162 m.p.h. at 8,000 ft.; cruising speed (70% power), 143 m.p.h., (65% power), 140 m.p.h., initial climb rate, 1,200 ft./min.; range (with 1,590-lb. payload), 680 mls.

Weights: Empty, 3,420 lb.; maximum loaded, 5,950 lb.

Accommodation: Pilot and maximum of nine passengers.

Status: Under development. First prototype was scheduled to fly late in 1967.

Notes: Owing much to the earlier single-engined PC-6 Porter and Turbo-Porter utility aircraft, the PC-8 Twin-Porter has been designed to supplement rather than replace its predecessors, offering similar short-take-off-and-landing characteristics and coupling these with the twin-engine safety factor. The PC-8 is claimed to be capable of taking-off at maximum gross weight at sea level under zero wind conditions within 525 ft. and clearing a 50-ft obstacle within 850 ft. Large freight-loading doors are provided in both sides of the fuselage, and a hatch is provided in the floor, and the standard wheel undercarriage may be replaced by skis or floats.

PILATUS PC-8 TWIN PORTER

Dimensions: Span, 51 ft. 2½ in.; length, 34 ft. 7¼ in.; height, 12 ft. 0 in.; wing area, 348 sq. ft.

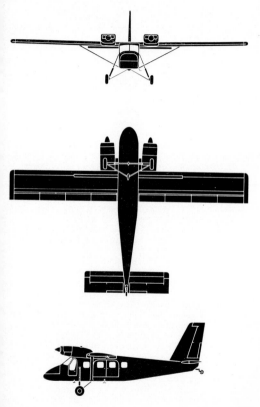

PIPER PA-28-180R CHEROKEE ARROW

Country of Origin: U.S.A.
Type: Light Cabin Monoplane.
Power Plant: One Lycoming IO-360 four-cylinder horizontally-opposed engine rated at 180 h.p.
Performance: Maximum speed, 170 m.p.h.; cruising speed at 75% power, 162 m.p.h.; initial climb rate, 875 ft./min.; service ceiling, 15,000 ft.; range at 75% power, 857 mls., at 55% power, 995 mls.
Weights: Empty, 1,380 lb.; loaded, 2,500 lb.
Accommodation: Four persons seated in pairs with individual front seats and bench-type rear seat. Baggage capacity of 200 lb. aft of cabin.
Status: In production. Cherokee Arrow added to the Cherokee range of light touring aircraft in June 1967.
Notes: The Cherokee Arrow is a retractable-undercarriage version of the current fixed-undercarriage PA-28-180 Cherokee D from which it differs also in having a fuel-injection engine. Both the Cherokee Arrow and Cherokee D differ from previous four-seaters in this series in having additional windows aft. The first Cherokee was flown on January 14, 1960 with the first production model following on February 10, 1961, the initial version being the PA-28-140 two-seater with a 140 h.p. Lycoming O-320-A2B engine. The PA-28-150, -160 and -180 Cherokee C were four-seaters respectively powered by the 150 h.p. O-320-E2A, the 160 h.p. O-320-D2A, and the 180 h.p. O-360-A3A, and the PA-32-260 Cherokee Six is a stretched six-seater with a 260 h.p. O-540-E4B5 engine.

PIPER PA-28-180R CHEROKEE ARROW

Dimensions: Span, 30 ft. 0 in.; length, 24 ft. 2½ in.; height, 8 ft. 0 in.; wing area, 160 sq. ft.

PIPER PA-31 NAVAJO

Country of Origin: U.S.A.

Type: Light Executive and Utility Transport.

Power Plants: Two Lycoming IO-540-K six-cylinder horizontally-opposed engines each rated at 300 h.p., or (Turbo Navajo) TIO-540-A1A six-cylinder horizontally-opposed engines each rated at 310 h.p.

Performance: (Figures in parentheses relating to Turbo Navajo) Maximum speed, 224 (260) m.p.h. at sea level (15,500 ft.); cruising speed at 75% power, 210 (247) m.p.h. at 6,400 (23,500) ft.; cruising speed at 55% power, 195 (209) at 14,600 (24,000) ft.; initial climb rate, 1,440 (1,395) ft./min.; service ceiling, 20,500 (26,300) ft.; range with normal reserves, 1,350 (1,525) mls. at 10,000 (20,000) ft.

Weights: Empty, 3,603 (3,759) lb.; maximum loaded, 6,200 (6,500) lb.

Accommodation: Cabin provides for three arrangements; standard six-seater, commuter version with eight seats, or executive version with separate crew compartment and four seats in main cabin.

Status: Prototype flown on September 30, 1964, with first production deliveries commencing 1967.

Notes: The largest aircraft in the Piper range until the appearance of the PA-35, the Navajo is produced in two versions, the basic model with IO-540-K engines and the Turbo Navajo with turbo-supercharged TIO-540-A1A engines.

PIPER PA-31 NAVAJO

Dimensions: Span, 40 ft. 8 in.; length, 32 ft. 7½ in.; height, 13 ft. 0 in.; wing area, 229 sq. ft.

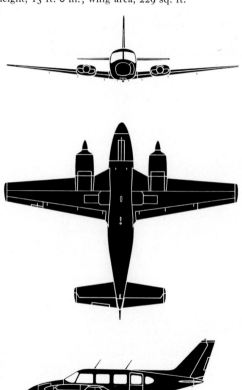

PIPER PA-35

Country of Origin: U.S.A.

Type: Light Commercial Feederliner.

Power Plants: Two Lycoming TIO-720 eight-cylinder horizontally-opposed engines each rated at 470 h.p.

Performance: (Estimated) Maximum speed, 242 m.p.h. at 10,000 ft.; cruising speed (at 75% power), 216 m.p.h. at 10,000 ft., 230 m.p.h. at 17,000 ft.; initial climb rate, 1,630 ft./min.; range (with 45 min. reserves), 650 mls. at 75% power, 810 mls. at 55% power.

Weights: Empty, 4,900 lb.; loaded, 9,000 lb.

Accommodation: Flight crew of two and maximum of 16 passengers. Alternative layouts available for 12 passengers or, in executive version, 11 passengers.

Status: Prototype scheduled to fly early 1968.

Notes: The largest aircraft yet built by Piper, the PA-35 is the result of a five-year market study, and has been built specifically to fulfil the requirements of the third-level scheduled-service, air taxi and light freighter market. Special provisions for cargo include a standard double door with the sill at truck-bed height to facilitate loading and unloading. The flight deck has been designed for one- or two-pilot operation, and features an external entry door, and standard fuel capacity is 166·5 Imp. gal., but the provision of auxiliary tip tanks is envisaged. The first production deliveries are scheduled for 1969.

204

PIPER PA-35

Dimensions: Span, 51 ft. 0 in.; length, 39 ft. 3 in.; height, 15 ft. 9 in.; wing area, 315 sq. ft.

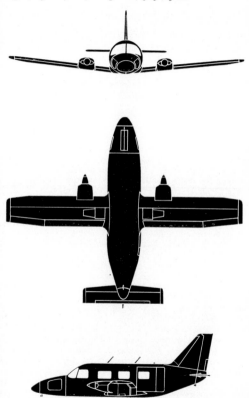

SAAB 35X DRAKEN

Country of Origin: Sweden.

Type: Single-seat Tactical Fighter-Bomber.

Power Plant: One Svenska Flygmotor RM 6C (Rolls-Royce RB.146 Mk. 60 Avon) rated at 12,710 lb.s.t. and 17,260 lb.s.t. with afterburning.

Performance: Maximum speed (without external stores), 1,320 m.p.h. at 36,000–40,000 ft. (Mach 2·0), initial climb rate (clean), 39,510 ft./min.; tactical radius (with nine 1,000-lb. bombs, 14 500-lb. bombs or four rocket pods) at high altitude at Mach. 0·9 including five min. combat at low altitude, 230 mls., at low altitude at 495 m.p.h., 150 mls., (with two 280 and two 110 Imp. gal. drop tanks plus two 1,000-lb. or four 500-lb. bombs), 700 mls. at high altitude and 400 mls. at low altitude; ferry range (with four 280 Imp. gal. drop tanks), 2,015 mls.

Weights: Maximum loaded, 35,270 lb.

Armament: Two 30-mm. Aden M/55 cannon and maximum external ordnance load of 9,000 lb.

Status: (Saab 35X) Under test. Current production versions for Swedish Air Force are the J 35F interceptor and S 35E tactical reconnaissance aircraft.

Notes: The Saab 35X is an export version of the basic Draken which, late in 1967, was being offered to Austria, Denmark, and other countries. Flown for the first time in the summer of 1967, the Saab 35X is optimised for the lo-lo-lo attack mission over extended ranges, and differs from the J 35F (see 1967 edition) in having additional internal tankage. Existing weapons hard points have been repositioned and provision made for additional hard points. The Saab 35X possesses secondary intercept capability.

206

SAAB 35X DRAKEN

Dimensions: Span, 30 ft. $10\frac{3}{4}$ in.; length (excluding nose probe), 46 ft. $10\frac{1}{4}$ in.; height, 12 ft. $8\frac{1}{3}$ in.; wing area, $529\cdot8$ sq. ft.

SAAB 37 VIGGEN

Country of Origin: Sweden.

Type: Single-seat (JA 37) Interceptor and (AJ 37) Strike Fighter, (S 37) Tactical Reconnaissance Aircraft, and (Sk 37) Two-seat Advanced Trainer.

Power Plant: One Svenska Flygmotor RM 8 (Pratt & Whitney JT8D-22) turbofan rated at approx. 16,000 lb.s.t. and 26,450 lb.s.t. with afterburning.

Performance: (Approximate) Maximum speed, 760 m.p.h. at 165 ft. (Mach 1·0), 1,320 m.p.h. at 39,370 ft. (Mach 2·0); time to 36,090 ft. at normal loaded weight, 2 min.; service ceiling, 60,000 ft.

Weight: Normal loaded, 35,275 lb.

Armament: (Attack mission) Rb 04C or Rb 05A attack missiles or pods containing six 13·5-cm. or 19 7·5-cm. rockets, or 30-mm. Aden cannon, or 1,000-lb. bombs on five external pylons. (Intercept mission) Rb 24, Rb 27 or Rb 28 AAMs.

Status: First of seven prototypes flown February 8, 1967, and second on September 21, 1967. Seventh prototype will be two-seat trainer. Initial production order calls for 83 AJ 37s and 17 Sk 37s. First delivery scheduled for July 1, 1971, with completion of initial order for 100 aircraft by beginning of 1974.

Notes: Versions of Viggen to be covered by follow-on contracts uncertain at time of closing for press when the future of both the S 37 reconnaissance model and JA 37 interceptor with secondary attack capability was under review.

208

SAAB 37 VIGGEN

Dimensions: Span, 34 ft. 9⅓ in.; length (including nose probe), 53 ft. 5¾ in.; height, 18 ft. 4½ in.

SAAB 105

Country of Origin: Sweden.

Type: Two-seat (SK 60A) Basic Trainer, (SK 60B) Light Attack, and (SK 60C) Reconnaissance and Attack Aircraft.

Power Plants: (Saab 105) Two Turboméca Aubisque (RM 9) turbofans each rated at 1,640 lb.s.t, or (Saab 105XT) two General Electric CJ610-4 turbojets each rated at 2,840 lb.s.t.

Performance: (Figures in parentheses relate to Saab 105XT) Maximum speed, 445 (604) m.p.h. at sea level, 454 (547) m.p.h. at 32,800 ft.; initial climb rate, 3,345 (12,795) ft./min.; time to 32,800 (29,530) ft., 17·5 (3·7) min.; range at 36,000 ft. at 403 (435) m.p.h., 1,210 (1,405) mls.

Weights: Empty, 5,534 (5,550) lb.; normal loaded, 8,800 (9,750) lb.; maximum, 9,920 (13,230) lb.

Armament: (Saab 105) Maximum external ordnance load of 1,650 lb., or (Saab 105XT) 4,400 lb.

Status: In production. (Saab 105) First prototype flown June 29, 1963 and first production example of August 27, 1965. Total of 150 ordered for Swedish Air Force of which approximately 90 delivered by beginning of 1968 when production rate was six per month. (Saab 105XT) Prototype flown April 29, 1967. Twenty ordered by Austria (as Saab 105O) with deliveries scheduled for mid-1969.

Notes: Saab 105 serves with Swedish Air Force with Aubisque engines and is offered for export (105XT) with CJ610-4 engines, The attack version of the Saab 105, the SK60B, has gunsight, gun-camera and armament pylon fasteners, and the reconnaissance-attack version, the SK 60C (illustrated) has a permanent reconnaissance camera installation in the nose.

SAAB 105

Dimensions: Span, 30 ft. 10 in.; length, 35 ft. 5¼ in.; height, 8 ft. 10¼ in.; wing area, 175·515 sq. ft.

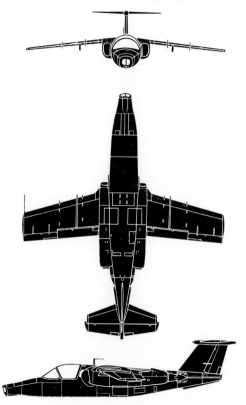

SHIN MEIWA PX-S

Country of Origin: Japan.
Type: Long-range Maritime Patrol Flying Boat.
Power Plants: Four General Electric T64-IHI-10 turboprops each rated at 2,850 e.s.h.p.
Performance: Maximum speed, 340 m.p.h.; normal cruising speed, 196 m.p.h. at 4,920 ft.; initial climb rate, 2,264 ft./min.; maximum ceiling, 29,530 ft.; normal range, 1,347 mls.; maximum range, 2,948 mls.
Weights: Operational empty, 51,852 lb.; maximum loaded weight, 86,862 lb.
Armament: Maximum of four 2,165-lb. homing torpedoes, six 5-in. HVAR missiles, or four 330-lb. depth bombs.
Status: First of two prototypes flown November 6, 1967. Production of 22 for Japan Maritime Self-Defence Force scheduled to commence 1969, deliveries starting 1971.
Notes: The PX-S employs an airscrew slipstream deflection system and boundary-layer control, a 1,250 s.h.p. T58-IHI-8B turboshaft being carried for the latter. The high length-to-beam ratio is claimed to provide exceptional seaworthiness, a groove-type spray suppressor evolved by the designer of the flying boat, Dr. Kikuhara, aiding operation in rough seas. Shin Meiwa is currently proposing a modified version of the PX-S to meet the AEW-X requirement for an airborne early warning aircraft. The PX-S has a normal crew complement of 12 members.
212

SHIN MEIWA PX-S

Dimensions: Span, 107 ft. 7⅓ in.; length, 109 ft. 10¾ in.;
height, 31 ft. 9¾ in.; wing area, 1,453·13 sq. ft.

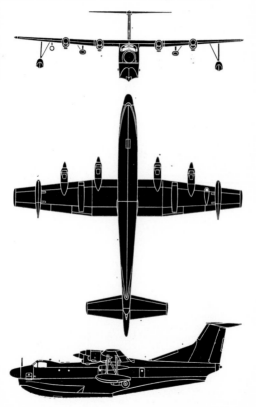

SHORT SC.5/10 BELFAST C. MK. 1

Country of Origin: United Kingdom.

Type: Military Strategic Transport.

Power Plants: Four Rolls-Royce Tyne R.Ty.12 Mk. 101 turboprops each rated at 5,730 e.h.p.

Performance: Maximum cruising speed (at 200,000 lb.) 352 m.p.h. at 28,000 ft.; economical cruising speed, 336 m.p.h. at 24,000 ft.; initial climb rate, 1,060 ft./min.; service ceiling, 30,000 ft.; range (30,000-lb. payload), 3,985 mls., (with max. payload—80,000 lb.), 1,000 mls. at 310 m.p.h. at 23,000 ft.

Weights: Basic operational, 127,000 lb.; maximum loaded, 230,000 lb.

Accommodation: Flight crew of four plus air quartermaster. Freight compartment capable of accommodating largest military vehicles. Typical military loads include three Alvis Saladin armoured cars, two Polaris-type missiles, three Wessex or four Whirlwind helicopters, or up to 80,000 lb. of freight for short-range tactical operations and 25,000 lb. in the strategic role. For the trooping role 150 troops may be carried, this number being increased to 250 by provision of complete upper deck.

Status: Production completed. First aircraft flown January 5, 1964. Tenth and last example rolled out late 1966.

Notes: Drag-reduction modifications on initial five aircraft delayed service introduction, but full-scale operation by No. 53 Squadron of the R.A.F.'s Air Support Command began in 1967.

214

SHORT SC.5/10 BELFAST C. MK. 1

Dimensions: Span, 158 ft. 9½ in.; length, 136 ft. 5 in.; height, 47 ft. 0 in.; wing area, 2,466 sq. ft.

SHORT SC.7 SKYVAN

Country of Origin: United Kingdom.
Type: Light Commercial Utility Transport.
Power Plants: (Srs. 2) Two Turboméca Astazou XII turbo-props each rated at 730 e.s.h.p., or (Srs 3) two Garrett-AiResearch TPE-331-201 turboprops each rated at 705 e.s.h.p.
Performance: (Astazou XII) Maximum speed, 236 m.p.h. at 10,000 ft.; maximum cruising speed, 207 m.p.h. at 10,000 ft.; economical cruising speed, 172 m.p.h.; initial climb rate, 1,450 ft./min.; service ceiling, 29,000 ft.; range (maximum fuel and 3,350-lb. payload), 720 mls., (maximum payload—4,600 lb.), 196 mls.
Weights: Basic operational, 7,350 lb.; maximum loaded, 12,500 lb.
Accommodation: Flight crew of two with accommodation for maximum of 18 passengers, or 12 casualty stretchers with medical attendants. In the freighter role up to 4,000 lb. of freight may be carried.
Status: In production. First production Series 2 aircraft flown October 29, 1965. First Skyvan with Garrett engines was scheduled to fly late 1967 with 10 flying by spring 1968.
Notes: Featuring a box-type fuselage with rear-loading facilities, the Skyvan is being produced with both Astazou XII and Garrett-AiResearch engines, being illustrated with the former above and with the latter on the opposite page. With the Garrett-AiResearch engines performance at take-off under all conditions is improved.

216

SHORT SC.7 SKYVAN

Dimensions: Span, 64 ft. 1 in.; length, 40 ft. 1 in.; height, 15 ft. 1 in.; wing area, 373 sq. ft.

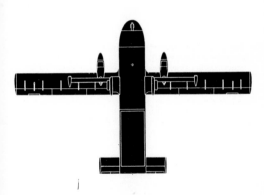

SIAI MARCHETTI S.208

Country of Origin: Italy

Type: Light Cabin Monoplane.

Power Plant: One Lycoming O-540-E4A5 six-cylinder horizontally-opposed engine rated at 260 h.p.

Performance: Maximum speed, 199 m.p.h. at sea level; cruising speed (75% power), 187 m.p.h. at 6,500 ft., (65% power), 176 m.p.h. at 8,200 ft.; service ceiling, 21,000 ft.; maximum range, 746 mls.

Weights: Empty, 1,720 lb.; loaded, 2,976 lb.

Accommodation: Basic accommodation for four persons in two pairs of side-by-side seats, with a collapsible seat installed in the baggage compartment for a fifth person.

Status: Prototype flown May 22, 1967. Initial series of 50 aircraft begun mid-1967 with production rate of four–five per month. First customer delivery was scheduled for November 1967.

Notes: The S.208 has been based on the lower-powered S.205 (see 1967 edition) and features individual rear seats in place of the bench of the earlier model, an optional fifth seat on which there are no weight restrictions, a third window on each side of the fuselage, electrical elevator trimming and electrically-operated flaps. Wingtip tanks are an optional extra which increase maximum range to 1,220 miles. A twin-engined derivative of the lower-powered S.205, the S.210, is currently under development.

218

SIAI-MARCHETTI S.208

Dimensions: Span, 35 ft. 7¾ in.; length, 26 ft. 3 in.; height, 9 ft. 5¾ in.; wing area, 173 sq. ft.

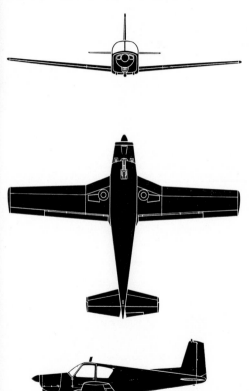

SIAI-MARCHETTI SF.260

Country of Origin: Italy.

Type: Light Cabin Monoplane.

Power Plant: One Lycoming O-540-E4A5 six-cylinder horizontally-opposed engine rated at 260 h.p.

Performance: Maximum speed, 230 m.p.h. at sea level; cruising speed (75% power), 222 m.p.h. at 6,500 ft.; (65% power), 210 m.p.h. at 8,200 ft.; initial climb rate, 1,770 ft./min.; service ceiling, 21,370 ft.; range, 1,050 mls.

Weights: Empty, 1,488 lb.; loaded (aerobatic), 2,200 lb., (utility), 2,425 lb.

Accommodation: Three persons in two side-by-side front seats and one person at rear.

Status: In production. First deliveries late 1966.

Notes: The prototype, known as the F.250 and powered by a 250 h.p. Lycoming O-540-A1D, was flown July 15, 1964, and was built by Aviamilano. The second prototype, built by SIAI-Marchetti and powered by an uprated engine, was designated SF.260 and appeared in 1966. The front seats have aerobatic-type safety belts, and the SF.260 is fully aerobatic with two persons and up to a gross weight of 2,200 lb., having one of the highest power-to-weight ratios of any current production light aircraft. The wingtip tanks are fixed, these having a capacity of 31 Imp. gal. as compared with the 22 Imp. gal. of the two wing tanks.

220

SIAI-MARCHETTI SF.260

Dimensions: Span, 26 ft. 11¾ in.; length, 23 ft. 0 in.; height, 8 ft. 6 in.; wing area, 108·5 sq. ft.

SIAT 223 FLAMINGO

Country of Origin: Federal Germany.
Type: Light Training and Touring Cabin Monoplane.
Power Plant: One Lycoming IO-360-C1A four-cylinder horizontally-opposed engine rated at 200 h.p.
Performance: Maximum speed, 158 m.p.h. at sea level; cruising speed (75% power), 152 m.p.h.; initial climb rate, 1,140 ft./min.; service ceiling, 15,750 ft.; maximum range, 840 mls.
Weights: Empty, 1,500 lb.; loaded, 1,985 lb.
Accommodation: Three persons in two side-by-side front seats with dual controls and one rear seat.
Status: In production. First of four prototypes flown spring 1967, and first production deliveries scheduled to commence 1968.
Notes: Produced by the Bölkow subsidiary, Siebelwerke ATG, the Flamingo was the winning design in a contest organised in 1962 for a standard club and training aircraft, and is currently proposed in several versions, these including the SIAT 223K fully-aerobatic two-seat trainer which is expected to be manufactured for Lufthansa and Swissair, the SIAT 223A two/three-seat utility aircraft, and the SIAT 223N four-seat tourer with enlarged cabin and extended wing. The Lycoming IO-320 engine of 160 h.p. is offered as an alternative to the O-360-C1A fuel-injection engine, and the aircraft is claimed to be suitable as an *ab initio* trainer for airline pilots and as a glider tug.

SIAT 223 FLAMINGO

Dimensions: Span, 26 ft. 10¾ in.; length, 24 ft. 4½ in.; height, 8 ft. 2⅓ in.; wing area, 122·385 sq. ft.

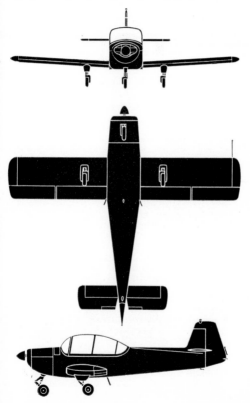

SUD-AVIATION CARAVELLE 11R

Country of Origin: France.

Type: Medium-range Commercial Passenger and Freight Transport.

Power Plants: Two Pratt & Whitney JT8D-7 turbofans each rated at 14,000 lb.s.t.

Performance: Maximum cruising speed, 498 m.p.h. at 24,600 ft., 490 m.p.h. at 27,430 ft.; range (with maximum payload—20,060 lb.), 1,430 mls., (with 16,500-lb. payload), 1,760 mls.

Weight: Maximum loaded, 114,640 lb.

Accommodation: Mixed passenger-freight with provision for 50 tourist-class passengers in rear cabin plus 656·7 cu. ft. cargo space in forward cabin and 581 cu. ft. in cargo hold. In all-passenger configuration a maximum of 89 tourist-class passengers may be carried.

Status: In production. The production prototype of the Caravelle 11R commenced trials on April 21, 1967 with delivery (to Air-Afrique) following in summer 1967. First of two prototype Caravelles flown on May 27, 1955, first production aircraft following on May 18, 1958. Production programme currently covers 250 Caravelle-series aircraft of which 245 had been ordered by November 1967 when production rate was two aircraft per month.

Notes: Caravelle 11R is derivative of 10R with large freight-loading door, strengthened freight floor, and a 36·6-in. additional section in forward fuselage. The Caravelle 11R has been delivered to Air Afrique and Air Congo, and some 230 Caravelles of all types were in airline service by the beginning of 1968.

224

SUD-AVIATION CARAVELLE 11R

Dimensions: Span, 112 ft. 6½ in.; length, 107 ft. 3¾ in.;
height, 28 ft. 7½ in.; wing area, 1,579 sq. ft.

SUKHOI SU-7M (FITTER)

Country of Origin: U.S.S.R.

Type: Single-seat Ground Attack Fighter.

Power Plant: One axial-flow turbojet rated at approximately 15,500 lb.s.t. and 22,050 lb.s.t. with afterburning.

Performance: (Estimated) Maximum speed (without external stores), 1,056 m.p.h. at 36,000 ft. (Mach 1·6), (with two 132 Imp. gal. drop tanks and two rocket pods), 790 m.p.h. (Mach 1·2); initial climb rate (without external stores), 30,000 ft./min., (high drag configuration), 23,500 ft./min.

Weights: (Estimated) Loaded (clean), 27,000 lb.; maximum overload, 30,500 lb.

Armament: Four 550-lb. bombs on external pylons (two beneath fuselage and two under wings), or two 550-lb. bombs plus two pods each housing 19 55-mm. rockets. Two 30-mm. cannon in wing roots.

Status: In production. Prototype allegedly flown 1955 and first production deliveries 1958–9.

Notes: The Su-7M is currently standard ground attack fighter equipment with the Soviet, Czech, Polish and Egyptian air arms, and a tandem two-seat training version, the Su-7UTI, is also in service. The Su-7 was evolved in parallel with Su-9 (Fishpot) all-weather delta interceptor, the two aircraft employing similar fuselages and tail surfaces married to wings optimised for the specific role of each model.

SUKHOI SU-7M (FITTER)

Dimensions: (Estimated) Span, 32 ft. 3 in.; length, 55 ft. 0 in.; height, 16 ft. 0 in.

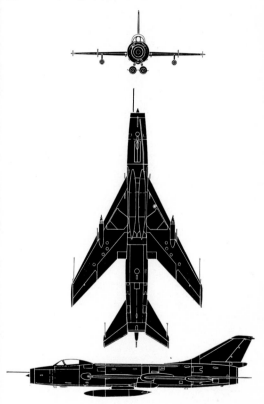

SUKHOI SU-7 (VARIABLE GEOMETRY)

Country of Origin: U.S.S.R.

Type: Variable Geometry Research Aircraft.

Power Plant: One axial-flow turbojet rated at approximately 15,500 lb.s.t. and 22,050 lb.s.t. with afterburning.

Performance: (Estimated) Maximum speed, 990 m.p.h. at 36,000–40,000 ft. (Mach 1·5); initial climb rate, 28,000–30,000 ft./min.; service ceiling, 50,000 ft.

Weights: Loaded, 29,000–30,000 lb.

Status: Experimental. Believed to have flown initially in 1966. Probably one or two examples constructed for basic research into the principles of variable-geometry wings.

Notes: Essentially a standard Su-7 ground attack fighter from the centreline out to the main undercarriage mountings, beyond which the outer wings have been replaced by new panels which give the original planform in fully swept configuration. The mid-span pivots and actuation mechanism are enclosed by fairings taking the form of combined fences and pylons, and presumably acting to prevent flow separations spreading outboard from the kink. Allegedly the first Soviet variable-geometry aircraft, the Su-7 conversion does not appear to have any production application, being devoted solely to basic research.

228

SUKHOI SU-7 (VARIABLE GEOMETRY)

Estimated Dimensions: Span (maximum sweep), 32 ft.
0 in., (minimum sweep), 46 ft. 0 in.; length (including
probe), 60 ft. 0 in.; height, 16 ft. 0 in.

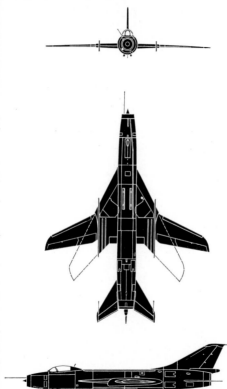

SUKHOI SU-9 (FISHPOT)

Country of Origin: U.S.S.R.

Type: Single-seat All-weather Interceptor Fighter.

Power Plant: One axial-flow turbojet of 15,500 (approx.) lb.s.t. and 22,050 (approx.) lb.s.t. with afterburning.

Performance: (Estimated) Maximum speed without external stores, 1,190 m.p.h. at 40,000 ft. (Mach 1·8), with two Anab or four Alkali AAMs, 990 m.p.h. (Mach 1·5); normal cruising speed, 570–600 m.p.h. at 36,000–40,000 ft.; initial climb rate, 27,000 ft./min.; time to 40,000 ft., 4·5 min.; service ceiling, 55,000 ft.

Weights: (Estimated) Loaded (clean), 25,500 lb.; maximum loaded, 29,000–30,000 lb.

Armament: Four Alkali or two Anab AAMs on underwing pylons.

Status: In production. Prototype of developed version illustrated was demonstrated publicly in 1961 and is believed to have supplanted earlier variants from 1965.

Notes: The Su-9 originally possessed some component commonality with the Su-7 (see pages 226–7), the fuselages and tail assemblies of the two aircraft being similar, but the latest service variant of this single-seat interceptor as demonstrated at Domodedovo on July 9, 1967, featured an enlarged air intake, and the nose centre-body had been enlarged and moved forward to produce a two-shock intake. The Su-9 is illustrated with two 132 (approx.) Imp. gal. drop tanks beneath the fuselage.

SUKHOI SU-9 (FISHPOT)

Estimated Dimensions: Span, 31 ft. 0 in.; length, 55 ft. 0 in.; height, 16 ft. 0 in.; wing area, 425 sq. ft.

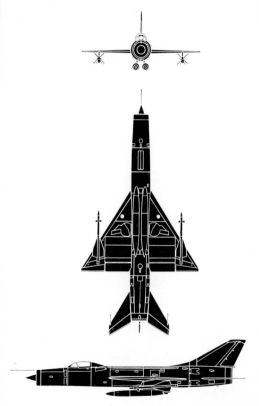

SUKHOI SU-11 (?) FLAGON-A

Country of Origin: U.S.S.R.

Type: Single-seat Interceptor Fighter.

Power Plants: Two turbojets each rated at approximately 15,500 lb.s.t. and 22,050 lb.s.t. with afterburning.

Performance: (Estimated) Maximum speed, 1,650 m.p.h. at 40,000 ft. (Mach 2·5), 910 m.p.h. at sea level (Mach 1·2).

Weights: Approximate loaded, 50,000–55,000 lb.

Armament: Two air-to-air missiles on underwing pylons, possibly of Anab type.

Status: In production. Believed first entered service with Soviet Air Force in 1966.

Notes: Presumably intended as a successor to the Su-9 and possibly designated Su-11, this twin-jet all-weather interceptor may be considered as, in effect, an enlarged and considerably refined development of the Su-9, much of the design of the earlier aircraft, including the cockpit enclosure, undercarriage, delta wing, airbrake location and vertical tail, being retained. A short-take-off-and-landing version of the basic design (illustrated above and dubbed Flagon-B) features two direct lift engines installed in the fuselage ahead of the propulsion units, two aft-hinged doors for these being provided in the upper fuselage decking, the exhaust outlets being covered by folding doors. In addition to the lift engine installation, the STOL version features extended outboard wing panels which, of reduced leading-edge sweep, result in a double-delta configuration.

SUKHOI SU-11 (?) FLAGON-A

Estimated Dimensions: Span, 33 ft. 6 in.; length, 71 ft.
0 in.; height, 16 ft. 0 in.

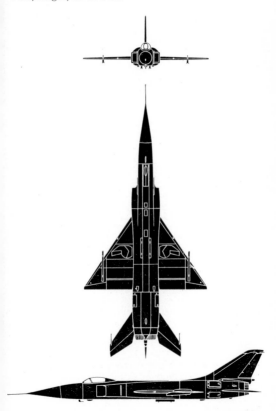

TED SMITH AEROSTAR 320-400

Country of Origin: U.S.A.
Type: Light Cabin Monoplane.
Power Plants: Two Lycoming IO-320 (IO-360) four-cylinder horizontally-opposed engines each rated at 160 (200) h.p.
Performance: (Data relates to Aerostar 320 with figures in parentheses referring to the Aerostar 400) Maximum cruising speed, 212 (220) m.p.h. at 10,000 ft.; initial climb rate, 1,613 (1,750) ft./min.; maximum range, 1,100 (1,245) mls.
Weights: Empty, 2,300 (2,400) lb.; normal loaded, 3,800 (4,000) lb.
Accommodation: Six passengers in pairs of side-by-side seats.
Status: Prototype development. The first prototype flown as Aerostar 320 in November 1966 and subsequently re-engined as Aerostar 400 and flown October 1967. Production scheduled to commence mid-1968.
Notes: The Ted Smith Aircraft Company has adopted a novel approach to the development of a light aircraft family which will be based upon three basic airframes —single and twin piston-engined, and twin jet—each with numerous common components, the structural design of the entire family being based on combinations and permutations of similar monocoque modules. Model 600 with 290 h.p. IO-540 engines flown October 21, 1967

TED SMITH AEROSTAR 320–400

Dimensions: Span, 35 ft. 0 in.; length, 34 ft. 0 in.;
height, 12 ft. 4¾ in.; wing area, 170 sq. ft.

TRANSALL C.160

Country of Origin: France and Germany.

Type: Medium-range Tactical Transport.

Power Plants: Two Rolls-Royce Tyne R.Ty.20 Mk. 22 turboprops each rated at 5,665 s.h.p. (6,100 e.s.h.p.).

Performance: Maximum cruising speed (at 90,390 lb.), 332 m.p.h. at 14,800 ft.; economical cruising speed, 308 m.p.h. at 26,250 ft.; service ceiling, 27,900 ft.; range (with maximum payload—35,280 lb., and 10% reserves plus 30 min.), 1,070 mls., (with maximum fuel and 17,640-lb. payload), 3,010 mls.

Weights: Operational empty, 61,843 lb.; normal loaded, 97,440 lb.; maximum, 108,250 lb.

Accommodation: Crew of four and 81 troops or 62 casualty stretchers and four medical attendants. Other possible loads include armoured vehicles, tanks and tractors not exceeding 35,270 lb. weight.

Status: In production. First of three prototypes flown February 25, 1963, and first of six pre-production aircraft on May 21, 1965. Current orders call for 160 production aircraft (50 C.160Fs for France and 110 C.160Ds for Federal Germany) of which first completed May 17, 1967. Planned maximum production rate is three per month with VFW and HFB in Germany assembling 54 and 53 respectively, and Nord-Aviation in France assembling 53, current orders being completed in 1972.

Notes: Joint Franco-German programme of which four production examples delivered by beginning of 1968. The 61e Escadre de Transport at Orléans-Bricy will convert to the C.160 by early summer 1968. Order for nine for South Africa negotiated 1966.

TRANSALL C.160

Dimensions: Span, 131 ft. 2½ in.; length, 105 ft. 3½ in.; height, 38 ft. 4¾ in.; wing area, 1,722·7 sq. ft.

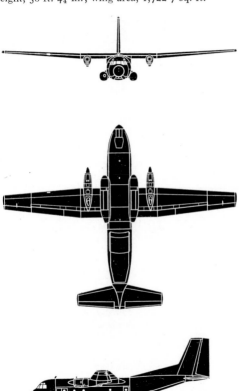

TUPOLEV TU-22 (BLINDER)

Country of Origin: U.S.S.R.

Type: Long-range Medium Bomber and Strike-reconnaissance aircraft.

Power Plants: Two turbojets rated at approximately 20,000 lb.s.t. and 27,000 lb.s.t. with afterburning.

Performance: (Estimated) Maximum speed, 990 m.p.h. at 40,000 ft. (Mach 1·5); maximum cruising speed, 630 m.p.h. at 40,000 ft.; unrefuelled tactical radius, 1,400 mls.; service ceiling, 60,000 ft.

Weights: Approximate loaded, 185,000 lb.

Armament: (Blinder-A) Free-falling weapons housed internally, or (Blinder-B) single semi-recessed Kitchen stand-off missile. Defensive: Single 23-mm. cannon in remotely controlled tail barbette.

Status: In production. Believed to have served with the Soviet Air Force since 1962–3.

Notes: Successor to the subsonic Tu-16 (Badger), the Tu-22 was originally evolved by the Tupolev design bureau in the mid 'fifties as the *Samolet "Yu"* with the design bureau designation Tu-105. The most recent examples of the Tu-22 seen embody a number of modifications, these including an extended flight refuelling probe and enlarged engine air intakes, nacelles and exhaust orifices. Camera windows are provided in the nose and aft, the standard crew complement comprises four members, and the tail gun is presumably intended to dispense a mixture of "chaff" and tracer to confuse the radar of interceptors and the guidance systems of missiles.

238

TUFOLEV TU-22 (BLINDER)

Estimated Dimensions: Span, 91 ft. 0 in.; length 133 ft. 0 in.; height, 17 ft. 0 in.; wing area, 2,030 sq. ft.

TUPOLEV (FIDDLER)

Country of Origin: U.S.S.R.
Type: Two-seat All-weather Interceptor.
Power Plants: Two turbojets of approximately 18,000 lb.s.t. and 22,000 lb.s.t. with afterburning.
Performance: (Estimated) Maximum speed, 925–990 m.p.h. at 40,000 ft. (Mach 1·4–1·5); maximum cruising speed, 630 m.p.h. at 40,000 ft. (Mach 0·95); normal tactical radius, 500–600 mls.; maximum unrefuelled range, 2,000 mls.; service ceiling, 60,000 ft.
Weights: Approximate normal loaded, 80,000 lb.
Armament: Four Ash AAMs.
Status: In production and in service.
Notes: Development of the Fiddler was initiated in the mid 'fifties as a scaled-down development of the Tu-98 (Backfin) of 1955, this being based on a Tu-16 (Badger) airframe with two axial-flow AL-7F engines installed in the fuselage. Current service models lack the ventral fins seen on the prototypes, these possibly having proved unnecessary at the modest supersonic speeds of which the Fiddler is capable.
240

TUPOLEV (FIDDLER)

Estimated Dimensions: Span, 56 ft. 0 in.; length, 85 ft. 0 in.; height, 20 ft. 0 in.

TUPOLEV TU-134A (CRUSTY)

Country of Origin: U.S.S.R.
Type: Short- and Medium-range Commercial Transport.
Power Plants: Two Soloviev D-30 turbofans each rated at 14,990 lb.s.t.
Performance: Maximum cruising speed, 572 m.p.h.; economical cruising speed, 528 m.p.h. at 32,810 ft.; range (with 15,432-lb. payload and one hour reserves at 88,185 lb.), 777 mls., (at 97,000 lb.), 1,490 mls., (with 11,023-lb. payload at 88,185 lb.), 1,180 mls., (at 97,000 lb.), 1,926 mls.
Weights: Empty equipped, 56,218 lb.; normal loaded, 88,185 lb.; maximum loaded, 103,616 lb.
Accommodation: Normal flight crew of three. Two versions are currently proposed, one accommodating 16 first-class and 48 tourist-class passengers, and the other accommodating 72 tourist-class passengers.
Status: In production. Prototype flown in second half of 1962. Five pre-production aircraft produced 1963–1964. First production deliveries (to Aeroflot) in 1966, and entered service in 1967.
Notes: Derived directly from the Tu-124 (and originally known as the Tu-124A), the Tu-134A has a similar fuselage cross section to that of its predecessor but there are now few common components between the two aircraft types. The Tu-134A employs a similar system of double-slotted flaps and air brakes to that of the Tu-124, and is also intended to operate from grass airfields. The responsible designers of the Tu-134A were L. Selyakov and A. A. Arkhangelskii.

242

TUPOLEV TU-134A (CRUSTY)

Dimensions: Span, 95 ft. 2 in.; length, 112 ft. 6 in.;
height, 29 ft. 7 in.; wing area, 1,238 sq. ft.

TUPOLEV TU-144

Country of Origin: U.S.S.R.

Type: Long-haul Supersonic Commercial Transport.

Power Plants: Four Kuznetsov NK-144 turbofans each rated at 28,660 lb.s.t. and 37,710 lb.s.t. with after-burning.

Performance: (Estimated) Maximum cruising speed, 1,550 m.p.h. at 49,200–65,600 ft. (Mach 2·35); service ceiling, 65,600 ft.; maximum ceiling, 68,900 ft.; maximum range, 4,040 mls.

Weights: Maximum loaded, 286,000 lb.

Accommodation: Basic flight crew of three and standard layout for 100 passengers in two cabins (forward cabin accommodating 18 passengers in three-abreast seating and aft cabin accommodating 82 in five- and four-abreast seating). Alternative layouts for 108 and 121 passengers.

Status: Prototype development. First of three proto-types scheduled to fly early 1968, with service introduction (by Aeroflot) 1970.

Notes: Designed to operate at similar speeds to those of the Anglo-French Concorde, the Tu-144 is claimed to be capable of operating at costs matching those of contemporary long-haul subsonic transports. Like the Concorde, it employs an ogival delta wing.

244

TUPOLEV TU-144

Dimensions: (Estimated) Span, 77 ft. 0 in., length,
190 ft. 0 in.; height, 37 ft. 0 in.

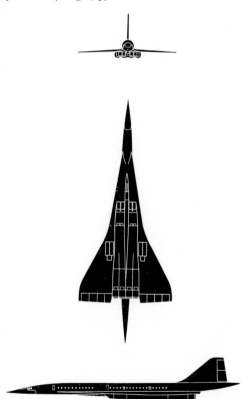

TUPOLEV TU-154

Country of Origin: U.S.S.R.

Type: Medium-range Commercial Transport.

Power Plants: Three Kuznetsov NK-8-2 turbofans each rated at 20,940 lb.s.t.

Performance: (Estimated) Maximum cruising speed, 564 m.p.h. at 39,370 ft.; economical cruising speed, 484 m.p.h.; range (with 35,840-lb. payload and 1 hr. reserves), 2,100 mls. at 550 m.p.h. at 36,000 ft., (with 23,520-lb. payload), 3,730 mls;. take-off distance (at 173,063 lb. to clear 50 ft.), 4,380 ft., (at 187,393 lb.), 4,920 ft.; landing distance (at 134,400 lb. from 50 ft.), 4,760 ft., (at 147,840 lb.), 5,100 ft.

Weights: Empty, 88,626 lb.; max. loaded (initial), 176,370 lb., (definitive), 189,598 lb.

Accommodation: Three crew members and 152 tourist-class passengers. Alternative versions provide accommodation for 164 economy-class passengers or 24 tourist- and 104 economy-class passengers. A proposed freighter variant will carry up to 56,000 lb. of cargo.

Status: Under development. Prototypes and pre-production aircraft under construction with first scheduled to fly 1967.

Notes: Intended as a successor to the Tu-104 in Aeroflot service, the Tu-154 is expected to commence route flying late 1968. Proposals call for a stretched version accommodating 220 for service from 1970–1.

TUPOLEV TU-154

Dimensions: Span, 123 ft. 2⅓ in.; length, 157 ft. 1¾ in.; height, 37 ft. 4¾ in.; wing area, 2,168·92 sq. ft.

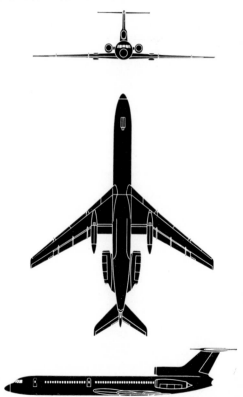

WASSMER SUPER 4-21 PRESTIGE

Country of Origin: France.
Type: Light Cabin Monoplane.
Power Plant: One Lycoming O-540-B2B5 six-cylinder horizontally-opposed engine rated at 235 h.p.
Performance: Maximum speed, 188 m.p.h. at sea level; cruising speed (75% power), 177 m.p.h. at 7,500 ft.; (65% power), 163 m.p.h. at 12,000 ft.; initial climb rate, 1,000 ft./min.; service ceiling, 16,000 ft.; normal range (standard tankage—49 Imp. gal.), 750 mls. at 65% power, (with optional supplementary tankage— 98 Imp. gal.), 1,550 mls.
Weights: Empty, 1,760 lb.; maximum loaded, 3,190 lb.
Accommodation: Five persons with two individual seats in front and rear bench seat for three persons.
Status: In production. Prototype Super 4-21 flown March 2, 1967.
Notes: The Super 4-21 Prestige is the latest derivative of the Wassmer WA-40 series of light cabin monoplanes introduced in 1960. The WA-40A Super 4 Sancy four/five-seater differed from the original WA-40 in having swept vertical tail surfaces and a lengthened fuselage nose, and the WA-41 Super 4 Baladou is essentially a simplified version of the Sancy with a fixed undercarriage and a similar 180 h.p. Lycoming O-360-A1A four-cylinder engine. Apart from its more powerful engine, the Super 4-21 Prestige differs from the Sancy in having an aerodynamically refined cockpit canopy, raised aft fuselage decking, and electrically-operated flaps and undercarriage retraction.

248

WASSMER SUPER 4-21 PRESTIGE

Dimensions: Span, 32 ft. 9½ in.; length, 25 ft. 9 in.; height, 9 ft. 5 in.; wing area, 172 sq. ft.

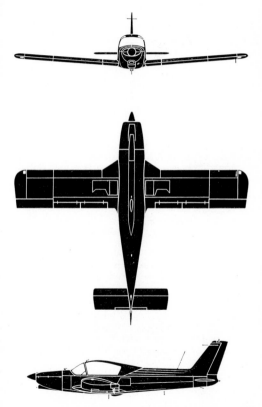

YAKOVLEV YAK-18T

Country of Origin: U.S.S.R.
Type: Light Cabin Monoplane.
Power Plant: One Ivchenko AI-14RF nine-cylinder radial air-cooled engine rated at 300 h.p.
Performance: Maximum speed, 186 m.p.h. at sea level; normal cruising speed, 155 m.p.h.; normal range, 480 mls.; maximum range, 620 mls.
Weights: Loaded, 3,572 lb.
Accommodation: Four persons in two side-by-side pairs, with full dual controls.
Status: In production. First deliveries believed late 1967.
Notes: Evolved from the tandem two-seat Yak-18A by Sergei Yakovlev, the Yak-18T features a new fuselage centre section, and a new wing centre section of extended span housing the inward-retracting main undercarriage members. Much of the basic Yak-18A structure has been retained, and the uprated AI-14RF engine similar to that installed in the single-seat aerobatic Yak-18PM (see 1967 edition) has been adopted for the new four-seat model. The Yak-18T may be adapted as a light freight transport, carrying a 550-lb. cargo load, and for the ambulance role a casualty stretcher and medical attendant may be carried. The Yak-18T is the latest derivative of the basic Yak-18 design which has been in continuous production for 20 years.

YAKOVLEV YAK-18T

Dimensions: Span, 36 ft. 7⅓ in.; length, 27 ft. 4¾ in.; height, 10 ft. 8 in.; wing area, 202·3 sq. ft.

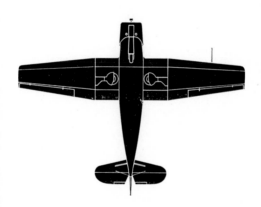

YAKOVLEV YAK-40 (CODLING)

Country of Origin: U.S.S.R.
Type: Short-haul Commercial Transport.
Power Plants: Three Ivchenko AI-25 turbofans each rated at 3,307 lb.s.t.
Performance: Maximum speed, 435 m.p.h.; maximum cruising speed, 373 m.p.h.; normal cruising speed, 342 m.p.h.; range (with 5,070-lb. payload and 45 min. reserves), 373 mls., (with maximum fuel and 2,425-lb. payload), 994 mls.
Weights: Normal loaded, 28,995 lb.; maximum loaded, 30,208 lb.
Accommodation: Basic flight crew of two and basic layout for 24 passengers in three-abreast seating or high-density layout for maximum of 31 passengers.
Status: In production. First prototype flown October 1966, with first deliveries (for Aeroflot) scheduled for 1968.
Notes: Intended primarily as a successor to the Li-2 (licence-built DC-3) in Aeroflot service, the Yak-40 places accent on maintenance simplicity and short-field capability. All three engines are operated on take-off, but the central engine may be throttled back to idle for fuel economy during cruise. All seats may be folded away and secured to the walls to give space for a 5,510-lb. cargo payload. Retractable airstairs are provided in the rear fuselage, and for simplicity there is a single services hydraulic system which operates the undercarriage, airstairs, nosewheel steering, tailplane setting gear and flaps.

252

YAKOVLEV YAK-40 (CODLING)

Dimensions: Span, 82 ft. 0¼ in.; length, 66 ft. 3 in.;
height, 20 ft. 11 in.; wing area, 753·473 sq. ft.

YAKOVLEV FREEHAND

Country of Origin: U.S.S.R.
Type: Single-seat Vertical Take-off and Landing Development Aircraft.
Power Plants: Two 7,000–9,000 lb.s.t. vectored-thrust turbofans.
Performance: Estimated maximum speed, 645 m.p.h. at sea level (Mach 0·85); maximum cruising speed, 500 m.p.h. at 5,000 ft. (Mach 0·8); tactical radius (VTOL), 100–150 mls. at sea level, (STOL), 150–200 mls.
Weights: Approximate max. (STOL), 18,000 lb.
Status: Believed experimental only. Possibly serving as basis for operational lightweight V/STOL strike and reconnaissance aircraft.
Notes: Publicly revealed at Domodedovo in July 1967 when two examples were seen, this vertical-take-off-and-landing aircraft has been attributed to the design bureau of Alexander Yakovlev, although its origin was not known with certainty at the time of closing for press. Of cropped-delta configuration with bicycle-type main undercarriage members and forward-retracting outrigger stabilising wheels, the aircraft has side-by-side turbofans exhausting through two swivelling nozzles at the centre of gravity. Stabilisation in hover is provided by four puffer pipes, one at each wingtip, one in the boom protruding from the nose, and one beneath the tail. It is to be assumed that in the case of failure of one turbofan the gas stream from the remaining powerplant can be ducted to both nozzles.

254

YAKOVLEV FREEHAND

Estimated Dimensions: Span, 27 ft. 0 in.; length (including 8 ft. nose boom), 53 ft. 0 in.; height, 13 ft. 0 in.

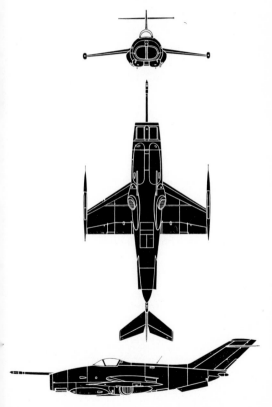

AGUSTA A 106

Country of Origin: Italy.
Type: Single-seat Light Anti-Submarine Helicopter.
Power Plant: One Turboméca-Augusta TAA 230 turboshaft rated at 320 s.h.p.
Performance: Maximum speed (at 2,866 lb.), 124 m.p.h.; maximum cruising speed, 115 m.p.h.; normal range, 174 mls.; maximum inclined climb rate, 1,220 ft./min.; hovering ceiling (in ground effect) 10,500 ft., (out of ground effect), 6,562 ft.
Weights: Empty, 1,300 lb.; loaded, 2,998 lb.
Dimensions: Rotor diameter, 31 ft. 2 in.; length overall, 36 ft. 0 in.; overall height, 8 ft. 2½ in.
Notes: The A 106, the prototype of which began its flight test programme early in 1966, is intended primarily for the anti-submarine warfare role for which it can carry two Mk. 44 torpedoes beneath the fuselage, but is also suitable for ground support missions for which it may be equipped with machine guns, guided anti-tank rockets, or fragmentation bombs. Other possible applications include the air ambulance task with a casualty stretcher on each side of the fuselage, or that of flying crane. The tubular skid landing gear is interchangeable with flotation bags, and an auxiliary fuel tank may be carried externally. The A 106 is a derivative of the A105B four-seater (see 1966 edition).

AGUSTA-BELL 204B

Country of Origin: Italy (under U.S. licence).
Type: Anti-submarine Warfare Helicopter.
Power Plant: One General Electric T58-GE-3 turboshaft rated at 1,325 s.h.p.
Performance: Maximum speed (at 7,500 lb.) 133 m.p.h. at sea level; maximum cruising speed, 119 m.p.h. at 1,000 ft.; maximum range, 295 mls.; maximum inclined climb rate, 1,960 ft./min. at 7,500 lb.; hovering ceiling (in ground effect), 15,000 ft., (out of ground effect), 9,500 ft.
Weights: Empty, 4,728 lb.; maximum loaded, 9,670 lb.
Dimensions: Rotor diameter, 48 ft. 0 in.; fuselage length, 41 ft. 7½ in.; overall height, 12 ft. 4½ in.
Notes: Agusta has manufactured the Bell Model 204B for the armed services of a number of countries, including those of Italy, the Netherlands, Norway, the Lebanon, Austria, Turkey, Spain, Saudi Arabia and Sweden, with the Bristol Siddeley Gnome H.1200, Lycoming T53-L-11 and General Electric T58-GE-3 turboshafts. Powered by the last-mentioned engine, a specialised anti-submarine warfare model has been developed by Agusta for use by Italy's *Marinavia*. It possesses auxiliary tanks for extended sonar missions of up to four hours, and can carry an armament of two Mk. 44 torpedoes.

R

BELL AH-1G HUEYCOBRA

Country of Origin: U.S.A.

Type: Two-seat Attack Helicopter.

Power Plant: One Lycoming T53-L-13 turboshaft rated at 1,250 s.h.p.

Performance: Maximum speed (at 8,624 lb.), 186 m.p.h.; cruising speed, 166 m.p.h.; normal range (at 8,624 lb.), 425 mls.; maximum inclined climb rate (at 8,624 lb.), 1,900 ft./min.; hovering ceiling (in ground effect), 18,600 ft., (out of ground effect), 11,900 ft.

Weights: Empty, 5,510 lb.; normal loaded, 8,624 lb.

Dimensions: Rotor diameter, 44 ft. 0 in.; fuselage length, 44 ft. 4¾ in.; overall height, 13 ft. 7¼ in.

Armament: One TAT-102 nose turret with one 7·62-mm. GAU-2B/A Minigun with 8,000 rounds, plus four XM-159 packs of 19 70-mm. rockets, four XM-157 packs of seven 70-mm. rockets, two XM-18 gun pods each with one 7·62-mm. Minigun, or six TOW wire-guided missiles.

Notes: The Model 209, or AH-1G, is currently entering U.S. Army service, and a total of 744 helicopters of this type had been ordered by the end of November 1967. The TAT-102 nose turret is to be supplanted by an XM-28 turret mounting both a Minigun and an XM-129 40-mm. grenade launcher.

258

BELL UH-1H IROQUOIS

Country of Origin: U.S.A.

Type: Utility and Transport Helicopter.

Power Plant: One Lycoming T53-L-13 turboshaft rated at 1,250 s.h.p.

Performance: Maximum speed (at 9,025 lb.), 138 m.p.h.; cruising speed, 136 m.p.h.; normal range (at 9,025 lb.), 327 mls.; maximum inclined climb rate, 1,760 ft./min.; hovering ceiling (in ground effect), 20,000 ft., (out of ground effect), 15,600 ft.

Weights: Empty, 4,850 lb.; normal loaded, 9,025 lb.

Dimensions: Rotor diameter, 48 ft. 0 in.; fuselage length, 42 ft. 0 in.; overall height, 14 ft. 6 in.

Notes: The UH-1H is the latest production version of the Model 205 Iroquois utility helicopter, and is essentially similar to the UH-1D apart from having a T53-L-13 turboshaft in place of the T53-L-11 derated to 1,100 s.h.p. The UH-1H can accommodate 12 troops, six casualty litters and a medical attendant, or 4,000 lb. of freight, and 553 examples of this variant of the Iroquois had been ordered by the end of November 1967. The UH-1D Iroquois is manufactured under licence in Italy and Federal Germany, and is distinguished from the earlier UH-1B primarily in providing greater cabin space. The Iroquois has been supplied to many air arms.

259

BELL MODEL 205A

Country of Origin: U.S.A.

Type: Commercial Transport Helicopter.

Power Plant: One Lycoming T53-L-13 turboshaft rated at 1,250 s.h.p.

Performance: Maximum speed (at 9,000 lb.), 138 m.p.h.; maximum cruising speed, 136 m.p.h.; normal range, 325 mls.; maximum inclined climb rate, 1,760 ft./min.; hovering ceiling (in ground effect), 20,000 ft., (out of ground effect), 15,600 ft.; service ceiling, 19,400 ft.

Weights: Normal loaded, 9,000 lb.

Dimensions: Rotor diameter, 48 ft. 0 in.; fuselage length, 42 ft. 0 in.; overall height, 14 ft. 6 in.

Notes: The commercial equivalent to the U.S. Army's UH-1H Iroquois utility helicopter, the Model 205A, deliveries of which are scheduled to commence early in 1968, can accommodate 14 passengers for air taxi or feederline services, and up to 10 passengers in a custom-built interior. Features of the Model 205A include wide sliding doors, " picture " windows, and a sound-conditioned cabin. Offering 220 cu. ft. of cabin space, the Model 205A replaces the earlier commercial Model 204B which has been on the market for some five years. Up to 4,000 lb. may be carried internally or 5,000 lb. as a slung load.

BELL MODEL 206A JETRANGER

Country of Origin: U.S.A.
Type: Five-seat Utility Helicopter.
Power Plant: One Allison 250-C18 turboshaft rated at 317 s.h.p.
Performance: Maximum speed, 150 m.p.h.; cruising speed (at 2,900 lb.), 134 m.p.h.; maximum inclined climb rate, 1,600 ft./min.; hovering ceiling (in ground effect), 8,800 ft., (out of ground effect), 4,200 ft.; range, 359 mls. at 137 m.p.h.
Weights: Empty, 1,295 lb.; loaded, 2,900 lb.
Dimensions: Rotor diameter, 33 ft. 4 in.; fuselage length, 28 ft. 2 in.; overall height, 9 ft. 6 in.
Notes: The JetRanger, the prototype of which was flown for the first time on January 10, 1966, is a commercial derivative of Bell's unsuccessful entry in the U.S. Army's LOH (Light Observation Helicopter) contest. Two additional prototypes have been used in the development programme, and the first production JetRanger deliveries were effected in January 1967. Lighter and faster than its LOH predecessor, the OH-4A, the JetRanger has an entirely redesigned fuselage with a refined structure resulting in a 155-lb. reduction in empty weight. The stabilising bar fitted to the OH-4A's rotor system has been deleted and the rotor mast extended.

261

BOEING-VERTOL CH-47C CHINOOK

Country of Origin: U.S.A.

Type: Medium Tactical Transport Helicopter.

Power Plants: Two Lycoming T55-L-11 turboshafts each rated at 3,750 s.h.p.

Performance: Maximum speed, 184 m.p.h. at 5,000 ft.; maximum radius of action (at 33,000 lb.), 214 mls.; maximum inclined climb rate, 2,740 ft./min.; hovering ceiling (out of ground effect), 13,850 ft.; service ceiling, 19,500 ft.

Weights: Empty, 20,026 lb.; normal loaded, 33,000 lb.; maximum loaded, 44,800 lb.

Dimensions: Rotor diameter (each) 60 ft. 0 in.; fuselage length, 51 ft. 0 in.; overall height, 18 ft. 6½ in.

Notes: First flown on October 14, 1967, the CH-47C supplants in production the CH-47B from which it differs solely in the model of the T55 turboshaft installed, the earlier variant of the Chinook having 2,850 s.h.p. T55-L-7C engines. The more powerful engines result in a 25 per cent increase in payload capability and enable the CH-47C to transport loads weighing up to 23,400 lb. The U.S. Army is scheduled to take delivery of the first CH-47C in March 1968, and by the end of 1967 more than 400 examples of the earlier CH-47A and -47B had been delivered. The Chinook first entered service in 1963.

BOEING-VERTOL CH-46D SEA KNIGHT

Country of Origin: U.S.A.
Type: Medium Transport and Assault Helicopter.
Power Plants: Two General Electric T58-GE-10 turbo-shafts each rated at 1,400 s.h.p.
Performance: Maximum speed (at 20,800 lb.), 166 m.p.h. at sea level; long range cruising speed (at 23,000 lb.), 153 m.p.h.; tactical radius, 115 mls.; maximum inclined climb rate (at 20,800 lb.), 1,900 ft./min.; hovering ceiling (at 20,800 lb. out of ground effect), 5,600 ft.
Weights: Empty, 13,067 lb.; max. loaded, 23,000 lb.
Dimensions: Rotor diameter (each), 51 ft. 0 in.; fuselage length, 44 ft. 10 in.; overall height, 16 ft. 11½ in.
Notes: The CH-46D and UH-46D are respectively U.S. Marine Corps logistic support and assault, and U.S. Navy medium utility and transport helicopters, these differing from the earlier CH-46A and UH-46A in having uprated turboshafts, cambered rotor blades with formation tip lights, provision for armour and armament, integral range fuel extension provisions, and, in the case of the UH-46D, a personnel rescue trans-fer boom. The CH-46D may accommodate up to 25 troops or 15 casualty litters and two medical attendants. More than 125 CH/UH-46s have been delivered.

BÖLKOW BÖ 105

Country of Origin: Federal Germany.
Type: Light Utility Helicopter.
Power Plants: Two MAN Turbo-6022-701-A3 turboshafts each rated at 375 s.h.p.
Performance: (Estimated) Maximum speed, 155 m.p.h.;
maximum cruising speed, 140 m.p.h.; maximum
inclined climb rate, 1,770 ft./min.; hovering ceiling (in
ground effect), 18,350 ft.; (out of ground effect),
13,100 ft.; service ceiling, 19,700 ft.; normal range, 280
mls., (with auxiliary fuel), 510 mls. at 6,600 ft.
Weights: Empty, 2,360 lb.; loaded, 4,410 lb.
Dimensions: Rotor diameter, 32 ft. 2 in.; fuselage
length, 28 ft. 0½ in.; overall height, 9 ft. 6 in.
Notes: The first prototype of the Bö 105 powered by
a pair of Allison 250-C18 turboshafts and equipped
with a Westland Scout articulated blade rotor system
was flown on February 16, 1967. This prototype was
destroyed as a result of ground resonance during
hover, and the second prototype differs in having
the Bölkow-developed rigid rotor system with lightweight glass-fibre-reinforced plastic blades. The
third prototype has MAN Turbo-6022-701-A3 engines
in place of the Allison 250-C18s. Production models
will be offered with both engine types.

BRANTLY MODEL 305

Country of Origin: U.S.A.

Type: Five-seat Utility Helicopter.

Power Plant: One Lycoming IVO-540-A1A six-cylinder horizontally-opposed engine rated at 305 h.p.

Performance: Maximum speed, 120 m.p.h. at sea level; economical cruising speed, 105 m.p.h.; maximum inclined climb rate, 1,300 ft./min.; hovering ceiling (in ground effect), 4,000 ft.; maximum range, 200 mls.

Weights: Empty, 1,840 lb.; loaded, 2,900 lb.

Dimensions: Rotor diameter, 28 ft. 8 in.; fuselage length, 24 ft. 5½ in.; overall height, 7 ft. 9½ in.

Notes: The Model 305 is essentially a stretched version of the two-seat Model B-2B, with a lengthened forward fuselage to accommodate two persons side-by-side in front and three on a bench seat aft, and a more powerful engine. The Model 305 was first flown in January 1964, production deliveries commencing in 1965, and during 1967 development of three turbine-powered derivatives was proceeding. These comprised versions of the Model 305 with single and twin 270 h.p. Allison 250-C18 turboshafts respectively, and the tandem-rotor 10-seat Model 2J10 with two Allison 250-C18 turboshafts or Boeing 550-1-12C turboshafts, and similar rotors and transmission systems, but prototypes had not commenced testing by the beginning of 1968.

265

FAIRCHILD HILLER FH 1100

Country of Origin: U.S.A.

Type: Four-seat Utility Helicopter.

Power Plant: One Allison 250-C18 turboshaft rated at 275 s.h.p.

Performance: Maximum speed, 127 m.p.h. at sea level; maximum cruising speed, 127 m.p.h. at 5,000 ft.; maximum inclined climb rate (at 2,530 lb.), 1,690 ft./min.; hovering ceiling (in ground effect), 15,950 ft., (out of ground effect), 11,100 ft.; service ceiling, 16,400 ft.; maximum range, 410 mls.

Weights: Empty, 1,395 lb.; max. loaded, 2,750 lb.

Dimensions: Rotor diameter, 35 ft. 5 in.; fuselage length, 29 ft. 9½ in.; overall height, 9 ft. 4¾ in.

Notes: The FH 1100 is a commercial derivative of the OH-5A which was the runner-up in the U.S. Army's LOH (Light Observation Helicopter) contest, and the first production model was rolled out in April 1966. A somewhat more sophisticated helicopter than the Hughes winning entry in the LOH contest, the FH 1100 has hydraulically-boosted cyclic and collective pitch controls, and has been test flown in level flight at 160 m.p.h., although for maximum turbine efficiency cruise and red-lined speeds are identical at 127 m.p.h. Basically a four-seater, the FH 1100 is also available in five-seater form.

HUGHES MODEL 500 (OH-6A) CAYUSE

Country of Origin: U.S.A.

Type: Four-seat Light Observation and Utility Helicopter.

Power Plant: One Allison T63-A-5A turboshaft rated at 252 s.h.p.

Performance: Maximum speed (at 2,400 lb.), 143 m.p.h. at sea level; economical cruising speed, 134 m.p.h.; maximum inclined climb rate, 1,560 ft./min.; hovering ceiling (out of ground effect), 7,600 ft.; service ceiling, 15,550 ft.; range, 413 mls.

Weights: Empty, 1,156 lb.; normal loaded, 2,400 lb.; maximum overload, 2,700 lb.

Dimensions: Rotor diameter, 26 ft. 3 in.; fuselage length, 23 ft. 0 in.; overall height, 8 ft. 8½ in.

Notes: The Model 500 was, in its military form (to which the above specification applies), pronounced winner of the U.S. Army's LOH (Light Observation Helicopter) contest in 1965, and deliveries commenced in September 1966 to meet an initial three-year commitment for 1,071 machines. The eventual U.S. Army requirement is estimated at 4,000 machines. Licence manufacture of the OH-6A is to be undertaken in Japan, and the OH-6A has been ordered by the Brazilian Air Force (20) and Navy (6). The commercial Model 500 is basically a five-seater.

KAMOV KA-25K

Country of Origin: U.S.S.R.

Type: General-purpose and Utility Helicopter.

Power Plants: Two Glushenkov turboshafts each rated at 900 e.h.p.

Performance: Maximum speed, 137 m.p.h.; normal cruising speed, 121 m.p.h.; normal range (with 12 passengers), 248 mls.; range with auxiliary fuel, 404 mls.; range with 4,410-lb. slung load, 31 mls.

Weights: Normal loaded, 15,653 lb.; maximum loaded, 16,094 lb.

Dimensions: Rotor diameter (each), 51 ft. 7½ in.; fuselage length, 32 ft. 3 in.; overall height, 17 ft. 7⅓ in.

Notes: A multi-purpose commercial helicopter evolved from the Ka-20 anti-submarine warfare helicopter, the Ka-25K was under test in prototype form in 1967. Capable of accommodating up to 12 passengers or a maximum freight load of 4,410 lb., the latter being slung beneath the fuselage, the Ka-25K featured an hydraulic winch, the winch operator being accommodated in an aft-facing glazed gondola beneath the fuselage nose. The turboshaft engines are mounted side-by-side above the cabin, and passengers are accommodated on tip-down seats arranged around the cabin walls. The three-blade co-axial rotors are power folded.

KAMOV KA-26 (HOODLUM)

Country of Origin: U.S.S.R.
Type: Light Utility Helicopter.
Power Plants: Two Vedeneev M-14V-26 air-cooled radial engines each rated at 325 h.p.
Performance: Maximum speed, 106 m.p.h.; cruising speed, 84 m.p.h.; economic cruising speed, 62 m.p.h.; hovering ceiling at 6,614 lb. (in ground effect), 4,068 ft. (out of ground effect), 2,625 ft.; service ceiling, 9,843 ft.; range (with seven passengers), 250 mls. at 1,640 ft., with auxiliary tanks, 746 mls.
Weights: Operational empty, 4,300 lb.; loaded, 6,614 lb., (agricultural version), 6,966 lb.
Dimensions: Rotor diameter (each), 42 ft. 8 in.; fuselage length, 25 ft. 5½ in.; overall height, 13 ft. 3 in.
Notes: The Ka-26, which appeared in 1965, is a multi-purpose helicopter which features a removable cabin for six passengers, two casualty stretchers, two sitting casualties and a medical attendant, or freight. The passenger cabin may be replaced by an open platform for bulky cargo loads, and an agricultural version can carry 1,984 lb. of dry chemicals or a tank for an equivalent quantity of liquid chemical. The plastic and fibreglass rotor blades are interchangeable. Production deliveries began in 1966.

269

LOCKHEED AH-56A CHEYENNE

Country of Origin: U.S.A.

Type: Two-seat Attack and Escort Helicopter.

Power Plant: One General Electric T64-GE-16 turbo-shaft rated at 3,435 s.h.p.

Performance: (Estimated) Maximum speed, 253 m.p.h. at sea level; cruising speed, 242 m.p.h. at 5,000 ft., 236 m.p.h. at 10,000 ft.; maximum inclined climb rate, 3,420 ft./min.; hovering ceiling (out of ground effect), 10,600 ft.; service ceiling, 26,000 ft.; maximum range, 875 mls.; ferry range, 2,890 mls. at 194 m.p.h.

Weights: Empty, 11,718 lb.; design loaded, 16,995 lb.; VTOL overload, 22,000 lb.; ferry overload (STOL), 28,000 lb.

Dimensions: Rotor diameter, 50 ft. 4¾ in.; wing span, 26 ft. 7¼ in.; wing area, 260 sq. ft.; fuselage length, 54 ft. 8 in.; overall height, 13 ft. 7¼ in.

Armament: One 7·62-mm. Minigun or 40-mm. grenade launcher in nose turret, and additional weapons on six 2,000-lb. capacity external pylons.

Notes: The Cheyenne was flown for the first time on September 21, 1967, and all 10 prototypes currently on order are scheduled for completion by mid-1968, U.S. Army evaluation commencing early in 1969. Between 500 and 1,000 AH-56As are to be acquired by the U.S. Army.

270

MIL MI-2 (HOPLITE)

Country of Origin: U.S.S.R.

Type: Light Utility Helicopter.

Power Plants: Two Izotov GTD-350 turboshafts each rated at 400 s.h.p.

Performance: Maximum speed, 143 m.p.h.; economical cruising speed, 112 m.p.h.; hovering ceiling (out of ground effect), 4,760 ft.; service ceiling, 13,120 ft.; range (with 1,984-lb. payload), 124 mls., (with auxiliary fuel), 444 mls.

Weight: Maximum loaded, 8,157 lb.

Dimensions: Rotor diameter, 47 ft. 6¾ in.; overall length, 57 ft. 1 in.; overall height, 11 ft. 0 in.

Notes: The Mi-2, which is currently in large-scale production in the Soviet Union and is manufactured under licence in Poland by WSK Swidnik, is being produced in four versions; a seven-passenger model, an agricultural model fitted with two external containers for a maximum of 1,984 lb. of dry chemicals, a freighter version with a 264-lb. capacity winch and the ability to carry 1,543 lb. internally or 1,764 lb. externally, and an ambulance with accommodation for four stretchers and one attendant. Initially flown in 1963, the Mi-2 has established two F.A.I.-recognised speed records for helicopters in its class, the latest, established on June 20, 1965, being 167·2 m.p.h.

271

MIL MI-6 (HOOK)

Country of Origin: U.S.S.R.
Type: Heavy Transport Helicopter.
Power Plants: Two Soloviev D25 turboshafts each rated at 5,500 s.h.p.
Performance: Maximum speed, 186 m.p.h.; normal cruising speed, 155 m.p.h.; range (with 13,228-lb. payload), 394 mls., (with 17,637-lb. payload), 385 mls., (with 26,455-lb. payload), 124 mls.; maximum range, 652 mls.; service ceiling, 14,764 ft.
Weights: Empty, 59,525 lb.; normal loaded, 89,287 lb.; maximum loaded, 93,696 lb.
Dimensions: Rotor diameter, 114 ft. 10 in.; fuselage length, 122 ft. 6 in.; overall height, 40 ft. 6 in.
Notes: First flown in 1957 and manufactured in some numbers since 1959, the Mi-6 is currently the world's largest helicopter, and is in service in both civil and military forms, the latter having been delivered to the U.A.R., North Vietnam, and Indonesia. The civil version can accommodate 65 passengers, and as an ambulance 41 casualty stretchers may be carried. The military version can accommodate 70 fully-equipped paratroops. Auxiliary wings are fitted to off-load the main rotor in cruising flight, but these may be removed when the Mi-6 is operated as a flying crane.

MIL MI-8 (HIP)

Country of Origin: U.S.S.R.

Type: Commercial Transport Helicopter.

Power Plants: Two Izotov TB-2-117 turboshafts each rated at 1,500 s.h.p.

Performance: Maximum speed, 155 m.p.h.; maximum cruising speed, 143 m.p.h.; normal cruising speed, 125 m.p.h.; range (with 6,614-lb. payload), 248 mls., (with 8,818-lb. payload), 62 mls.; maximum range, 280 mls., (with auxiliary fuel), 435 mls.; service ceiling (at 24,251 lb.), 13,120 ft.

Weights: Empty, 15,800 lb.; normal loaded, 24,251 lb.; maximum loaded, 26,455 lb.

Dimensions: Rotor diameter, 56 ft. 5 in.; fuselage length, 49 ft. 2½ in.; overall height, 14 ft. 9 in.

Notes: Evolved from the piston-engined Mi-4 but retaining few interchangeable components in its definitive production form, the Mi-8 is being manufactured in two versions, one accommodating up to 28 passengers and the other being intended for the freight transportation role with a maximum cargo load of 8,818 lb. Either passenger or freight version may be converted for the ambulance role with 12 casualty stretchers and one medical attendant. A controllable winch and underside cargo hook for lifting slung loads up to 5,500 lb. may be fitted.

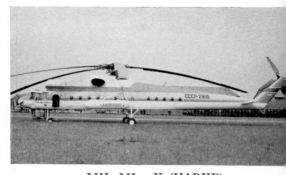

MIL MI-10K (HARKE)

Country of Origin: U.S.S.R.
Type: Heavy Crane-type Helicopter.
Power Plants: Two Soloviev D25V turboshafts each
rated at 5,500 s.h.p.
Performance: (Specification is applicable to standard
Mi-10 but, apart from range, is also generally applicable to the Mi-10K) Maximum speed (with empty
cargo platform), 124 m.p.h., (with high-density platform load weighing 26,455 lb.), 112 m.p.h.; range (with
26,455-lb. load), 155 mls.; maximum range (with
auxiliary fuel), 391 mls.; service ceiling, 9,842 ft.
Weights: (Mi-10) Empty, 59,525 lb.; maximum loaded,
95,790 lb.
Dimensions: Rotor diameter, 82 ft. 0 in.; overall length,
137 ft. 5 in.; overall height (Mi-10), 32 ft. 6 in.
Notes: The Mi-10K, which was still undergoing
development in 1966, is a derivative of the production
Mi-10 (see 1966 edition) in which a supplementary
cockpit with full controls is provided beneath the front
fuselage, the height of the undercarriage has been
reduced, and maximum slung load is increased to
24,250 lb.; this being scheduled to be raised to 30,864
lb. with an increase in rated power of the D25V turboshafts to 6,500 s.h.p.
274

SIAI-MARCHETTI SH-4

Country of Origin: Italy.

Type: Three-seat Light Utility Helicopter.

Power Plant: One Franklin 6A-350-D or -D1 six-cylinder horizontally-opposed engine derated to 160 h.p.

Performance: Maximum speed, 100 m.p.h. at sea level; maximum cruising speed, 87 m.p.h.; economic cruising speed, 80 m.p.h.; maximum inclined climb rate, 1,140 ft./min.; hovering ceiling (in ground effect), 12,300 ft., (out of ground effect), 6,730 ft.; service ceiling, 13,155 ft.; maximum range, 186 mls.

Weights: Empty, 1,120 lb.; maximum loaded, 1,900 lb.

Dimensions: Rotor diameter, 29 ft. 7½ in.; fuselage length, 25 ft. 1¼ in.; overall height, 9 ft. 9¼ in.

Notes: The first prototype SH-4 helicopter was flown in March 1965, this being followed by five production examples completed in 1967 when work began on an initial series of 50 helicopters of this type with first deliveries scheduled for 1968. Design emphasis has been placed on simplicity of operation, ease of maintenance and low initial cost. The standard tubular-steel skid undercarriage may be replaced by multi-cell floats, agricultural spraying equipment may be fitted, and an external stretcher pod may be attached to the port side of the fuselage. An external sling can support loads up to 440 lb.

275

SIKORSKY SH-3D SEA KING

Country of Origin: U.S.A.
Type: Amphibious Anti-submarine Warfare Helicopter.
Power Plants: Two General Electric T58-GE-10 turbo-shafts each rated at 1,400 s.h.p.
Performance: Maximum speed, 166 m.p.h.; maximum cruising speed, 148 m.p.h.; long-range cruising speed, 133 m.p.h.; maximum inclined climb rate, 2,200 ft./min.; hovering ceiling (out of ground effect), 6,500 ft.; service ceiling, 14,700 ft.; maximum range (with 10% reserves), 624 mls.
Weights: Empty, 11,865 lb.; loaded, 18,626 lb.
Dimensions: Rotor diameter, 62 ft. 0 in.; fuselage length, 54 ft. 9 in.; overall height, 15 ft. 4 in.
Notes: The current production version of the Sea King for the U.S. Navy, the SH-3D has been delivered to the Spanish Navy, and is being manufactured under licence in Italy by Agusta for the Italian Navy, and in the U.K. by Westland for the British Navy. The British version is powered by the Bristol Siddeley H.1400 coupled Gnome, has British-designed electronic equipment, and is scheduled to enter service with the British Navy in 1969. A Sikorsky-built SH-3D airframe re-engined with the British power plant flew for the first time on September 8, 1967.

SIKORSKY HH-3E

Country of Origin: U.S.A.
Type: Medium Rescue Helicopter.
Power Plants: Two General Electric T58-GE-5 turbo-shafts each rated at 1,500 s.h.p.
Performance: Maximum speed, 165 m.p.h.; maximum cruising speed, 154 m.p.h.; maximum inclined climb rate, 1,520 ft./min.; service ceiling, 11,700 ft.; range (with external jettisonable fuel tanks), 748 mls.
Weights: Empty, 14,426 lb.; normal loaded, 19,500 lb.; maximum, 22,050 lb.
Dimensions: Rotor diameter, 62 ft. 0 in.; fuselage length, 56 ft. 7 in.; overall height, 18 ft. 1 in.
Notes: The HH-3E is an armoured rescue variant of the S-61R, and differs from the U.S.A.F.'s CH-3E support transport helicopter in having self-sealing fuel tanks, a retractable flight refuelling probe, defensive armament and a rescue hoist. The HH-3F of the U.S. Coast Guard is similar but does not have armour, armament or self-sealing tanks. It features sophisticated electronic gear for automatic navigation, communications, and search and weather radar. The HH-3F can carry 20 passengers or nine casualty stretchers, and the CH-3E can accommodate up to 30 troops or 5,000 lb. of cargo.

277

SIKORSKY HH-53B

Country of Origin: U.S.A.

Type: Combat Aircrew Rescue Helicopter.

Power Plants: Two General Electric T64-GE-3 turbo-shafts each rated at 3,080 s.h.p.

Performance: Maximum speed, 195 m.p.h.; cruising speed, 172 m.p.h.; maximum inclined climb rate, 1,625 ft./min.; service ceiling, 18,550 ft.; maximum range, 806 mls.

Weights: Empty, 23,125 lb.; normal loaded, 35,000 lb.; maximum overload, 42,000 lb.

Dimensions: Rotor diameter, 72 ft. 2¾ in.; fuselage length, 67 ft. 2¼ in.; overall height, 24 ft. 10½ in.

Notes: Flown for the first time on March 15, 1967, the HH-53B is the U.S.A.F. combat aircrew rescue version of the S-65, and features a retractable flight refuelling probe, jettisonable auxiliary fuel tanks, rescue hoist and defensive armament. Armament comprises three 7·62-mm. Miniguns firing from a port forward window, a starboard door and the tail hatch. The CH-53A Sea Stallion is a U.S. Marine Corps heavy assault helicopter which can accommodate up to 37 combat-equipped troops, 24 casualty stretchers, or such loads as two Hawk missiles or a 105-mm. howitzer and carriage. The CH-53A is powered by two 2,850 s.h.p. T64-GE-6 turboshafts and first flew on October 14, 1964.

278

SUD-AVIATION SA-321 SUPER FRELON

Country of Origin: France.
Type: Medium Transport and (SA-321G) Anti-submarine Warfare Helicopter.
Power Plants: Three Turboméca Turmo IIIC.3 turboshafts each rated at 1,500 s.h.p.
Performance: Maximum speed (at 24,250 lb.), 146 m.p.h. at sea level; maximum cruising speed, 130 m.p.h.; maximum inclined climb rate, 2,500 ft./min.; service ceiling, 15,750 ft.; range (with 5,925-lb. payload), 234 mls.; ferry range, 770 mls.
Weights: Empty, 13,558 lb.; normal loaded, 24,250 lb.; maximum loaded, 26,455 lb.
Dimensions: Rotor diameter, 62 ft. 0 in.; fuselage length, 62 ft. 3 in.; overall height, 22 ft. 0 in.
Notes: Two prototypes and four pre-production examples of the SA-321 Super Frelon (Super Hornet) are currently being followed by 38 production examples, including six examples of the non-amphibious transport version for the Israeli Defence Force/Air Force. The amphibious ASW version, the SA-321G, is being manufactured for France's Aéronavale (12) and the South African Air Force (15), this having Sylph radars in the outrigger floats, dunking sonar, and up to four homing torpedoes and other ASW stores. The commercial SA-321F (illustrated) flew on April 7, 1967.

279

SUD-AVIATION SA-330

Country of Origin: France.

Type: Tactical Assault and Logistic Transport Helicopter.

Power Plants: Two Turboméca Turmo IIIC.4 turboshafts each rated at 1,300 s.h.p.

Performance: Maximum speed, 174 m.p.h. at sea level; normal cruising speed, 157 m.p.h.; maximum inclined climb rate, 1,635 ft./min; hovering ceiling (out of ground effect), 12,800 ft.; service ceiling, 18,300 ft.; range (with 3,858-lb. payload), 230 mls.; ferry range, 870 mls. at 4,900 ft.

Weights: Empty, 7,187 lb.; normal loaded, 13,220 lb.; maximum loaded, 14,110 lb.

Dimensions: Rotor diameter, 49 ft. 2½ in.; fuselage length, 45 ft. 6 in.; overall height, 17 ft. 0 in.

Notes: The SA-330 has been developed specifically to a French Army requirement, and quantity production will be initiated during 1967. The SA-330 has a crew of two and accommodates a maximum of 12 fully-equipped troops, and seven test and evaluation examples had joined the flight development programme by late 1966, the first having flown on April 15, 1965. Plans currently call for the manufacture of 130 SA-330s under the 1965–70 Loi Programme. Forty-eight helicopters of this type are to be acquired by the United Kingdom.

SUD-AVIATION SA-340

Country of Origin: France.
Type: Light Observation Helicopter.
Power Plant: One Turboméca Astazou IIN turboshaft rated at 630 s.h.p.
Performance: Maximum speed, 164 m.p.h.; maximum cruising speed, 152 m.p.h.; hovering ceiling (out of ground effect), 10,826 ft.; range with 1,305-lb. payload, 186 mls. at 4,920 ft.
Weights: Empty, 1,675 lb.; loaded, 3,527 lb.
Dimensions: Rotor diameter, 32 ft. 9½ in.; overall length, 29 ft. 1¼ in.; overall height, 8 ft. 4¾ in.
Notes: Flown for the first time on April 7, 1967, the SA-340 has been adopted as the standard light observation helicopter for both the French and British armed forces. In the British Army the SA-340 will supplant the Bell Sioux, and the British requirement is for some 600 helicopters of this type, the French requirement being for approximately 100. The SA-340 will attain operational status in 1969, and a pre-production series of four helicopters is scheduled to be completed during the spring of 1968. The definitive version will differ from the prototype (illustrated) in having a vertical tail surface housing a shrouded rotor, this supplanting the horizontal stabiliser and endplate fins.

281

WESTLAND SCOUT A.H. MK. 1

Country of Origin: United Kingdom.
Type: Light Utility Helicopter.
Power Plant: One Bristol Siddeley Nimbus 102 turbo-shaft rated at 685 s.h.p.
Performance: Maximum speed, 132 m.p.h.; maximum cruising speed, 122 m.p.h.; maximum inclined climb rate, 1,700 ft./min.; hovering ceiling (in ground effect), 15,400 ft., (out of ground effect) 10,000 ft.; maximum range (with standard fuel), 322 mls.
Weights: Empty, 3,184 lb.; maximum loaded, 5,300 lb.
Dimensions: Rotor diameter, 32 ft. 3 in.; fuselage length, 30 ft. 7½ in.; overall height, 8 ft. 11 in.
Notes: Derived from the same basic design as the Wasp A.S. Mk. 1, the Scout is currently in production for and in service with the British Army, two have been supplied to the Royal Australian Navy, one to the Bahrein State Police, two to the Uganda Police Air Wing, and three to the Royal Jordanian Arab Army. For the ambulance role two casualty stretchers may be accommodated, and a sling for external freight and a power-operated rescue hoist may be fitted. The Scout may also carry wire-guided missiles such as the Nord SS.11, and up to five passengers may be carried. A number of components are similar to those of Wasp.

WESTLAND WASP A.S. MK. 1

Country of Origin: United Kingdom.
Type: Anti-submarine Warfare Helicopter.
Power Plant: One Bristol Siddeley Nimbus 503 turbo-shaft rated at 710 s.h.p.
Performance: Maximum speed, 121 m.p.h.; cruising speed, 110 m.p.h.; maximum inclined climb rate, 1,440 ft./min.; hovering ceiling (in ground effect), 12,500 ft., (out of ground effect), 8,800 ft.; maximum range, 303 mls.
Weights: Empty, 3,452 lb.; maximum loaded, 5,500 lb.
Dimensions: Rotor diameter, 32 ft. 3 in.; fuselage length, 30 ft. 5¾ in.; overall height, 9 ft. 9 in.
Notes: The Wasp A.S. Mk. 1 currently serves with the Royal Navy in the anti-submarine weapon-carrying role, operating from platforms aboard frigates equipped with long-range asdic. In this role the Wasp is normally crewed by a single pilot and carries two 270-lb. torpedoes. Dual controls may be fitted for the training role, and four passengers may be carried. The Wasp has been supplied to the Brazilian, Netherlands, New Zealand and South African navies. A specially designed undercarriage incorporating fully castoring, lockable wheels permits normal operation aboard ship in heavy seas, and a power hoist, operated by the pilot or a crewman, is installed for rescue missions.

283

WESTLAND WESSEX MK. 60

Country of Origin: United Kingdom.
Type: Commercial Transport and Utility Helicopter.
Power Plants: Two Bristol Siddeley Gnome turboshafts each rated at 1,350 s.h.p.
Performance: Maximum speed, 132 m.p.h.; economical cruising speed, 121 m.p.h.; maximum inclined climb rate, 1,350 ft./min.; service ceiling, 10,000 ft.; maximum range (standard tankage), 311 mls.
Weights: Empty equipped, 8,657 lb.; maximum loaded, 13,500 lb.
Dimensions: Rotor diameter, 56 ft. 0 in.; fuselage length, 48 ft. 4½ in.; overall height, 16 ft. 2 in.
Notes: The Wessex 60 is the civil counterpart of the R.A.F.'s Wessex H.C. Mk. 2, and will accommodate a maximum of 16 passengers, normal accommodation providing for a crew of two and 10 passengers. Alternatively, the Wessex 60 may accommodate eight casualty stretchers and two ambulatory casualties plus a medical attendant. Derived from the Sikorsky S-58, the Wessex has been manufactured in a number of versions with either two Gnome engines or a single Napier Gazelle, a current model with the latter being the Wessex H.A.S. Mk. 3 anti-submarine warfare helicopter (see 1967 edition) which will eventually be supplanted in Royal Navy service by the SH-3D Sea King.

INDEX OF AIRCRAFT TYPES

Made and Printed in Great Britain by
Butler & Tanner Ltd., Frome and London
722.1167